Desert Journey

Desert Journey

a memoir

Vera Marie Verna

LEONINE PUBLISHERS
PHOENIX, ARIZONA

Copyright © 2024 Vera Marie Verna

All rights reserved. No part of this book may be reproduced or transmitted in any form or by any means, electronic or mechanical, including photocopying, recording, or by any information storage or retrieval system now existing or to be invented, without written permission from the respective copyright holder(s), except for the inclusion of brief quotations in a review.

Published by

Leonine Publishers LLC
Phoenix, Arizona, USA

ISBN-13: 978-1-942190-71-4
Library of Congress Control Number: 2024912973
10 9 8 7 6 5 4 3 2 1

Visit us online at www.leoninepublishers.com
For more information: info@leoninepublishers.com

Dedicated to
Sister Philip Marie Burle
9/21/1933 - 4/4/2022
Long time friend and a spiritual director who guided me, a single mother, with my three children for thirty-one years.

Picture of Mother Teresa with Sister Burle, retreat director for Mother Teresa's sisters in Calcutta in 1991.

Contents

FOREWORD 1

CHAPTER 1
   WOMB EXPERIENCE/DAY CARE/
   NOTRE DAME/JOIN ARMY 3

CHAPTER 2
   FIRST MARRIAGE/RETURN TO US
   VIA THE PAN-AMERICAN HIGHWAY 31

CHAPTER 3
   WALKERS CAY/PRESIDENT NIXON/
   PLANE CRASH 49

CHAPTER 4
   PROMISED TRIP TO EUROPE 59

CHAPTER 5
   THE SURPRISE DIVORCE/
   DISCONNECT FROM GOD 71

CHAPTER 6
   SECOND MARRIAGE/ANTHONY'S
   DISAPPEARANCE 81

CHAPTER 7
   HIGHWAY TO HELL/BORN AGAIN/
   FIRST ADOPTION..................99
CHAPTER 8
   HI NELLA, SINGLE PARENTS MINISTRY/
   MOTHER AND CHILD ART GALLERY.......125
CHAPTER 9
   SECOND ADOPTION/MOTHER TERESA/
   SISTER PHILIP MARIE BURLE............175
CHAPTER 10
   GRANDPA PETER.....................203
CHAPTER 11
   THIRD ADOPTION/MOTHER TERESA/
   THE CARMELITES 223
CHAPTER 12
   JOURNEY UPDATE 30 YEARS LATER/
   FEEDING PREGNANT AND SENIOR LAMBS..243
CHAPTER 13
   CONCLUSION.......................263

Foreword

Vera Marie Verna's journey was long and hard, and best described by poet Mary Stevenson.

>FOOTPRINTS IN THE SAND
>One night I dreamed I was walking along the beach with The Lord. Many scenes from my life flashed across the sky. In each scene I noticed footprints in the sand. Sometimes there were two sets of footprints.
>This bothered me because I noticed that during the low period of my life, when I was suffering from anguish, sorrow or defeat, I could see only one set of footprints. So I said to the Lord, "You promised me Lord, that if I followed you, you would walk with me always. But I have noticed that during the most trying periods of my life there has only been one set of footprints in the sand. When I needed you most, you have not been there for me?"
>The Lord replied, "The times when you have seen only one set of footprints, is when I carried you."

CHAPTER 1

Womb Experience/Day Care/ Notre Dame/Join Army

I recently found a book in my extensive formal library that my mother had read around the time she birthed me 79 years ago. She had told me that this, her first pregnancy, was difficult and performed by a midwife at a downtown Philadelphia Retreat for pregnant women. She said there were no sonograms or spinal shots at the disposal of these midwives at the time. Only natural birthing was offered.

The book was by Charles Dickens and was entitled *Bleak House*; it was not one that I have read. As I opened it, I thought, *Where did this book come from? How did it get into my library?* The hard cover was taped and had lots of loose pages. When I opened it, the first page was very loose but still attached. Mother had written on this page in pencil: "Preston Retreat, 19th and Hamilton St., Spring Garden. Baby

Vera Verna was born September 23, 1943. Black hair and very pretty! Nurses well and smiles for Mommy-1943." She continued, "Mothers Birthday 21st now 19 years old Daddy brought flowers and sent me candy and fruit." (I was told he was drafted into the Army when I was born and while we were living at my grandparents' home in Philadelphia.)

For many years after my birth, my mother and grandparents told me that I experienced recurring nightmares, but only when I was sick with high temperatures. (Early childhood illnesses like chickenpox). Mother told me that back then there was no easy access to antibiotics or family doctors for the poor.

I was told that when I was sick with high temperatures I would scream out suddenly. When someone came to check on me and bent over the crib, I would scream even louder. When I learned to talk I would suddenly shout out, "Get away, bad bear. No, bad bear!" The same nightmare continued into my early teens. I was able to ask my mother a lot of questions and recount more details such as: "It was very hot and dark. It was something like a sliding board or tunnel with pressure on both sides."

Mom told me she was in labor for a very long time. When the heat became intense, I would hear the question: "Who do you choose?" On one side was a growling, scary bear-like beast. The other side was a vague figure with an aura of beauty and goodness.

As I grew older, I realized that, in terror of the ugly growling beast, I had rushed to embrace the beautiful image of goodness. About a year ago, I asked a spiritual director about a bible reading we were sharing, Isaiah 49, concerning verse 1, "The Lord called me from the womb, from the body of my mother. He knew my name." I told the spiritual director that I was delivered by a midwife in a home for indigent mothers and that in 1943 there was not much technology available. I was told that I had a long and difficult delivery. I told her about the question I was asked: "Who do you choose?" I related about the nightmares I experienced. She said, "Wow, really?" She had heard that there were reports by people (now adults) who were told their births were traumatic, life-threatening births and those survivors recounted that they too heard the same question: "Who do you choose?" I proceeded to search every site I could find that reported physical or spiritual experiences in the womb. I discovered physical, scientific reports such as those caused by loss of oxygen during delivery. The reports stated such loss of oxygen could affect the brain and be irreversible, noting some forms of depression and other effects to those who survived a traumatic or life threatening birth. I downloaded a 17-page pastoral letter by the Most Reverend Salvatore Joseph Cordileone, Archbishop of San Francisco, from May 2021, entitled: *Before I Formed You in the Womb I Knew You* (Jer 1:5). I noted the resources he included. One was entitled *Life Before Birth* by author Marjorie A. England, 2nd edition (United Kingdom: Mosby-Wolfe, 1996). It contained a list of references of modern embryology pertaining to life before birth.

I went on to research the Preston Retreat in Philadelphia and spoke to the Catholic Historical Society and the Philadelphia Historical Society. The Preston Retreat was a maternity house in 1866 for married women of indigent circumstances. The retreat house was open to "women of good character." A pregnant woman would have to provide testimonials of "good character." The records stated that these women would be serviced by midwives at no charge.

The records further stated that the wealthy women of Philadelphia had the privilege of delivering in their own homes with their own midwives. Apparently philanthropy was in vogue in the 1800s. In 1831, Stephen Girard left the city of Philadelphia $6 million to provide a private K-12 boarding school for poor male orphans. The Preston Retreat was funded by Dr. James Preston, a Philadelphia physician. Also, the Holy Family Center was donated and is now vacant with the land owned by the Archdioceses of Philadelphia.

Mother Teresa of Calcutta provided for those pregnant mothers and their children. Abortions in India are especially high and target female babies. Mother Teresa notified the hospitals not to destroy the babies, especially the females. She would take them to her orphanage and would put them up for adoption. She would search the high dump heaps in the streets of Calcutta for babies and bring them to her orphanage as well. She would then bring the babies to New York for those who could not travel to India at no charge! (Like myself, who many years later would ask the Missionaries of Charity to do the same for me as I was trying to adopt a three-year-old little girl.

My mother was severely anemic when she became pregnant with her third child and was told to stay in bed, where she was unable to care for myself and my little brother. I was four years old and my little brother two years old when we were placed in a Catholic day care. Dad would drop us off at the day care near the church for poor families, which was staffed by Catholic nuns. Mom told me to keep an eye on my little brother, Nick, to make sure he did not get hurt on the playground and check if his diaper needed to be changed. I was already doing that at our rental apartment. We lived on the second floor of an old row house. (The roof had no guardrails or fences and it had a makeshift patio, which was the only area for us to be outside.) I was required to stay in the playpen to be sure he was safe. I loved taking care of him from the moment he arrived. I learned with trial and error to change his diaper, dress, and feed him.

At the day care center, he was in a room with 1-3 year olds. I was in another room with 4-5 year olds. I had lunch on a very long, narrow table with many children facing each other and alongside. The menu was always the same. It consisted of homemade soups every day with lots of veggies and lima beans (the only protein we had), a piece of bread, and a glass of milk. If we finished our soup and bread, we could have red Jell-O and only then were we allowed out to play! My playground time was the same as my little brother's and I was happy to keep an eye on him. I loved the soup. Mom was not a cook so I lapped up the bowl quickly and then ate my bread. I was the first to be ready for the red Jell-O. Most of the children on this long, narrow table did not like lima beans. They deposited them into my clean bowl! The cook would come in to say, "Okay, you can all have Jell-O now and go out to play, but not Vera until she finishes all her beans!" I would protest every day, saying they were not mine, that I ate all of mine and cannot eat any more! So there I sat, no Jell-O, and no going out to play. I was worried about my little brother. Finally, the cook saw me crying after a week of this. She was observant and believed me, marking the end of that trial. Now out to play and care for my little brother. I would catch him taking off his diaper before going down the sliding board. We never went to parks or had access to sliding boards. I guess he thought this was required. The caregivers were amused that I was so concerned.

They immediately took him inside for a new diaper. I would not see him again until the end of the day. We were always the last to get picked up, waiting for Dad to bring us home. Little brother was in a crib in another room. I would sit by the reception entrance in a large wood chair. I remember my feet did not touch the ground and I would swing my feet back and forth, trying to wait patiently for Dad to pick us up. I would see a nun going by me as it started to become late. She always had some cleaning items in her hands. One day I asked her "Where are you going?" She said, "I am going to clean the chapel." I asked her, "What is chapel?" The nun answered, "Jesus lives in the chapel." I replied, "Can I go to the chapel with you to see Him? I could help you clean." She said, "No thank you. You have to wait for your father. He should be here soon."

My grandfather would talk a lot about Jesus when I lived with my grandparents; for a while I was their first and only grandchild. I was told Dad was in the Army. Grandpa asked my Aunt Marie, his youngest child, to walk me to Sunday morning Mass. He would give me a nickel to put into the collection basket. I was told later that he went to the earliest Mass alone. I loved going to Mass at the big old church. Grandpa said Jesus lived there too.

At 5 ½ years old, I was approved to go to the first grade at that same church day care school. Mom had a little girl walk me to school, and afterwards, I would be picked up by my dad or the little girl would walk me home to our apartment. I remember that by the end of the first week I could read! That day I bolted out of the school and started walking to my grandparents' home which was close by. I knew the way. I brought my First Reader with me. I ran into their house shouting, "I can read! Look at my book, I can read!" Well, there were no phones back then for them to call my parents, who were frantically looking for me. I don't remember how they finally found me at my grandparents' home. Grandpa tried to talk them out of a consequence. It was not a serious one, they just shouted loudly. The rest of my life they would not raise their voice to correct or punish me because I would start to cry and would become very hurt for hours. The family would say, "She is so sensitive!" When I could not fall asleep for the required nap time at home with little brother (I was told that I was never able to take a nap), I was asked by my mother to leave the room. I would leave with one of my books and go off to another room to read. Reading was such an adventure! I could not get enough books to read.

    I was happy when I found the school library had an abundance of books there. I read all I could find for my reading level and beyond. The family moved from our South Philadelphia apartment to a small house that my grandfather built for us. It was a two story and had room for us as we were now three, soon to become six, children. Dad helped him, but Grandpa, who was master carpenter at the Philadelphia Navy Yard, did most of the work. This was exciting.

We had a large lot with plenty of trees too. It was quite a change from our city apartment. Grandpa created a swing area and the few neighbors were very friendly. My brother and I now had friends our age living across the street. We were sent to the nearby Catholic school. It was quite a change living in the suburbs but we loved it. After a few years we moved to Media, Pennsylvania. Dad was laid off from his Westinghouse job and soon left home to run a tavern at the New Jersey shore. The house in Media was a two bedroom, one bath home. Again my grandfather came to the rescue. There was a huge stand-up attic with wood stairs going up to the attic. Luckily, there was a window on each side for air circulation as it was not heated and had no air conditioning. We were grateful for the air circulation.

Grandpa finished the attic with one side for boys and the other for girls. He built closets at both ends for our clothes and belongings. We slept dormitory style with the two boys on one side and the three girls on the other side of the stairwell (which was the only access to our room). When our little brother Patrick arrived, his nursery was in the second downstairs bedroom next to the master bedroom. With such close accommodations it is a wonder we did not argue more, but we were able to make the adjustment from the two story that Grandpa built with not much complaining.

    I was able to go to the all-girls Notre Dame High School in Media. It had a magnificent huge campus with Notre Dame of France details. I was accepted in 1958 with prepaid tuition from our local Catholic church. I enjoyed the nuns, who were excellent teachers, especially my English teacher who encouraged me to write a lot of essays and promoted me at the end of Freshman Year for the English award.

    My father was not around much as he was living at the Jersey Shore running his tavern and dating. My mother went to work at a local department store in downtown Media. She was dating after work as well. I would walk a mile and a half to Notre Dame. When school was out, I would walk home quickly to take care of my five brothers and sisters to cook for them and get them ready for bed. There was not much money for food. The local parish priest would come to the house every week to bring food. He would also check report cards as I was on paid tuition by our church. My brother attended an all-boys Catholic school with his tuition paid by the church as well. We both always had all A's. My brother left home after the second year of high school. I thought the conditions at home were too much for him. He was under age for most jobs, but he did so well for himself! He was quickly promoted to management positions for each job. I was very proud of him but I missed him! I admired his desire to go on his own. He surprised everyone with his determination to succeed no matter what!

    I knew I had to finish high school and be there for my brothers and sisters. We were now six children and myself the eldest. The pastor of our Catholic church would bring rice and beans, canned tuna— and of course loaves of bread— along with peanut butter and jelly. I tried to make the canned food as appetizing as possible. No hot dogs or hamburgers here! The kids were hungry but sometimes the same meals of tuna fish, rice, and beans were not enough. Because we could not afford the school lunches, we would take peanut butter and jelly sandwiches to school, so dinners of the same were not well received. I would tell them if they ate their dinner and took their shower, I would allow them to watch Disney's Mickey Mouse Club. We had a small television but they didn't mind. They loved singing the Mickey Mouse song with Annette Funicello, the lead musketeer. There was only one bath downstairs. I would have them stand in line, single file. One by one, all five would rush to get dressed for bed and be ready for the Mickey Mouse show. When baby Patrick arrived later, I would help care for him in his nursery downstairs. They would go to bed right after watching their favorite program. Sometimes if they had a hard time falling asleep, I would rock them in our rocking chair.

    We would always say grace before meals. It was routine to say, "Dig in!" at the end of the prayer, but not until we blessed ourselves in the name of the Father, Son, and Holy Spirit. Even on those rare occasions when our dad would come to visit and take us out for pizza on Sunday, we would say the prayer, cross ourselves, and say, "Dig in!"

Mom would drive us to church on Sunday. We would sit together at the rear of the church. One Sunday when the priest made the sign of the cross for the final blessing, in the name of the Father, the Son, and Holy Spirit, my little brother, Tommy, shouted out, "Dig in!" Everyone turned to look at us and of course they had no idea what that was all about. We would joke about that years later.

My little brother, Tommy, died and I gave his eulogy at the funeral. I recounted the events of his life and his struggle to keep up with the rest of us, as he had some severe learning disabilities and was not considered as successful as the others in the family. He had come to live with me in Florida for a short while. I tried to find him work as a master carpenter, but he was not able to keep a job for long. He was always so grateful and enjoyed my cooking for him. He would help wash and dry the dishes and was consistently helpful.

At the end of the eulogy, I made the sign of the cross saying aloud, "In the name of the Father, the Son, and the Holy Spirit, little brother dig in now at the banquet table of the Lord!" After graduating from Notre Dame

High School, I was fortunate to secure a good paying job in downtown Philadelphia. The family moved from Media, Pennsylvania, to South Jersey. I would catch a ride with a kind neighbor to the bus stop and then the train would take the subway to downtown South Philadelphia. The job paid well. I enjoyed my favorite food, which was not the famous Philly Cheese Steak, but of all things I would order a large tuna sub! This was half for breakfast and half for lunch.

    I decided that it would be a good idea to enroll at the renowned downtown Pierce Business School. I found out they offered night classes and enrolled immediately in their one-year program. After work, I would take the subway to business school. My dinner was Philly Pretzels with lots of mustard. The Notre Dame nuns taught me well with stenography and typing, but I thought to extend my business training as it appeared that my best job opportunities at present were in business. I liked Pierce Business, with their excellent teachers who were quick to explain business procedures, present different skills, and introduce new terminology that I would have to utilize. I knew nothing of business except what the Notre Dame nuns taught me. I was soon to finish their one-year program when one evening, as I was walking to school, I noticed a sign that said "JOIN THE ARMY AND SEE THE WORLD." I was still undecided about where I belonged. The Notre Dame nuns thought I might have a calling to become a nun. I thought I should check out the Army and call the Recruiting Center. I was undecided about whether to marry, become a nun, go to college, or consider business opportunities after I graduated from Pierce Business School. I arrived at the Recruiting Center and introduced myself. I told the recruiter that I was working downtown as a stenographer and would soon graduate from Pierce Business School the following week. I told him that if I joined the Army, I did not want to wear a uniform. (I wore uniforms for 14 years at Catholic school). He smiled and said, "Okay, that would make you a civilian Army employee." He said he would have to do testing in order to offer me employment. He set up a test for stenography and typing. Thanks to the Notre Dame nuns, I passed with flying colors! He offered me Vietnam, Thailand, or Panama. I told him I wanted Europe. He explained that I would have to work out of the United States for two years before I could work in Europe. I chose Panama since I had taken four years of Spanish at Notre Dame and I had an aunt, who I had never met, living in Panama. I called my aunt (after locating her number) to tell her I was accepted by the Army to work in Panama and planned to arrive soon. She told me that just recently she had contacted my mother and her sister living in Philadelphia to invite myself and my cousin to visit her!

She was told that my cousin could not come to visit at this time and that my mother was undecided about the invitation. She told me to call her and she would pick me up at the airport. She was very happy about my opportunity to work in Panama. I had never traveled and soon found out about passports, shots, and how to book my flight.

I only had enough money for a one-way ticket and booked it. My parents were very upset and did not want to offer me assistance. I knew nothing about Panama and decided to go to the fantastic library in downtown Philadelphia to learn about the country. Unfortunately, all the books I chose were all about the building of the canal and showed pictures of people wearing khaki-colored clothing and living in small tents. The books cited that people were dying of malaria! I went out to purchase a suitcase and filled it with mosquito spray for the mosquitoes and to protect me from mosquitoes! I was a very naive 19 year old and thought I would just have to persevere with my plan regardless of the malaria threat!

My brother had introduced me to his young friend in my senior year. He was a senior as well who went to a very fine public school nearby. I was not allowed to date, so sometimes he would pick me up from school with a pizza and we would go to a local cemetery to eat it. No chance I would be seen there!

Donald was very attentive and concerned for me, as he knew from my brother what my conditions at home were like. When we would meet in the cemetery, he said he would like to marry me and wanted to build us a wonderful two-story home to live in. He was always respectful and kind. No cell phones then, so contact was limited. Donald asked his mother to bring a heart jewelry set (heart-shaped earrings and necklace) over to my house. I was not at home and my mother answered the door. She handed my mother the gift, told her to give it to me, and that it was from Donald. When I arrived home, my mother asked, "Who is Donald?"

I don't know how I was finally able to convince her to give me the gift; she wanted me to give it back to him. When it was time to leave, I said tearful goodbyes and said I would write to them.

Since my parents were against my joining the Army, I had no one to drive me to the New York airport. Donald borrowed his mother's car and drove me to the airport. When we said goodbye, I thanked him for being such a good friend and hoped he would understand that I needed to be on my own to figure out what direction in life was right for me.

The desire to become a nun, as suggested by Notre Dame, was high on my list of options. When I arrived in Panama, I had to go through Customs. When they opened my suitcase and saw all the spray cans of aerosol mosquito repellent, they said "What is this? How did you ever get past Customs in New York with all these aerosol cans!"

I told them I checked my one bag in New York and knew nothing about flying procedures. I explained that I thought I needed protection from the mosquitoes, which were causing Malaria here. The customs agent said, "We don't have a problem with malaria anymore," and that I would not need my bug spray!

He gave me a look that would have sent me back home immediately, but I was so determined to "find myself." My aunt picked me up at the airport and she was surprised when I told her what was in my suitcase. I was told that I would have to check in with the Canal Zone. Within a short time, I was taking my required physical and was told to be on standby as they tried to find a suitable placement for me as I was told there were several positions open in the Canal Zone.

After a long wait (my aunt's husband hired me to work in his office so that I would have some cash), the Army eventually assigned me to the engineering department. Since I had nothing but khakis and the few dresses my aunt's dressmaker had made for me, I was grateful for all the help I could get to make a presentable appearance for this job. I was told that there were no department stores in Panama or in the Canal Zone. I found out that even the Army commissaries on base had no clothing.

There were no Sears, Walmarts, or Jordan Marsh stores here. What did I know? I never shopped for clothes. I wore uniforms to school and had very few clothes that were appropriate for church and my job in Philadelphia. When I reported to my job, the Lt. Colonel referred me immediately to his wife. He could see I was struggling with clothes and my general presentation. He told her that I was very qualified for what he needed from a secretary. Stenography and typing skills were especially needed for his many meetings that were top security. I received my security clearance and would be able to handle it along with other non-security assignments. General maintenance requests were assigned to the engineering department. He said he knew that I was very young, naïve, and "just out of the box"! I will never forget what he told his wife. Help her she is as "just out of the box." I am sure his wife wondered how I even got there! I told her my aunt had a dressmaker and his wife recommended appropriate clothing to the dressmaker.

I was told everyone in the Republic and the Canal Zone had to travel to Miami to buy their appropriate attire, and not just clothing. She told me that not even the Army commissaries had clothing. Most army families would take shopping trips to the US as well as the residents of Panama.

My aunt referred me to a dressmaker and a few outfits were made in a hurry. My first two months on the job found me inundated with required paper work. Copies were sent out here and there as well as so many copies of the engineers' directives and summary reports. I thought them to be redundant and wrote a letter suggesting X amount of dollars that could be saved by sending only half of the copies! They handed me an award for that suggestion and gave me a $30.00 check (back then it was a lot of money).

It was presented to me as an "Efficiency Award" in front of all the employees and officers. I thought, "So much fuss for a suggestion for saving a little money?"

My salary was tax free, more money than I thought I could ever earn. I decided I would buy a new car. The fact that I did not know how to drive or had never been behind the wheel of a car, never entered my mind. I went right out to a car dealer in the Republic and purchased a new Chevy that would be delivered to the tax-free side on the other side of Panama. I purchased the new Chevy and when the dealer asked me if I wanted to try one out with a test drive, I said, "No, I will order this one." (I did not say I never drove a car.) I don't remember the model.

I told him I wanted the blue one, just like the one he showed me, with four doors. I went to the library to check out a book on how to drive a car. There were no driver's education classes and no one offered classes on how to drive a car. I was notified that the new car arrived in the free zone. I was able to get a ride to the other side. There was only one road from the Atlantic to the Pacific and I was sure I could find my way back. I had my receipt showing I paid for the car and they went to get it.

I was asked if I wanted them to drive it to the parking lot out front. I said yes thinking I would practice in the parking lot before I headed back on the only road that went from the Atlantic to the Pacific. I sat in the car and opened the book. It took a while before I realized that the car was left with the emergency brake on as it was on an incline. I found that out and went on to Chapter 2: How to drive with a stick shift. Well it is hard to believe now that I attempted to find the gear shifts to drive it and did not know until Chapter 3 that I had purchased an automatic transmission! I practiced in the parking lot and then headed back to the other side. I was okay until I got to the city. Panama was like Rome (when I went there). No one paid attention to stop signs or traffic lights, and they drove fast. I thought this was normal and drove like everyone else did to keep up. I made friends with some of the young Panamanians who were planning to go to the US to study. They practiced their conversational English and I practiced my conversational Spanish.

    I would drive them around to the local hang-out spots since they were my age but did not drive. I became popular with the locals and was invited to their parties and boat trips around the city. I discovered the Island of Tobago with them. They called me the "Gringita." The colonel thought I should continue further with conversational Spanish and sent me to the University of Panama to take classes. The nuns taught me how to read Spanish but I needed to improve my conversational Spanish. I remember going out to lunch in the Republic of Panama for the first time. The menu was in Spanish and was not specific about ordering eggs. When the waiter came around to take my order, I said in Spanish that I wanted the thing that came out of the chicken! He said in Spanish, "Oh, *huevos*. How do you want them?" I motioned whatever. I was introduced to something similar to *huevos rancheros*, which to this day is my preference. My conversational Spanish at the University of Panama helped and I practiced with my friends too. Within no time I was speaking like a native.

Rooftop playpen with little brother

Historical Notre Dame graduation

CHAPTER 2

First Marriage/Return to US via the Pan-American Highway

A young man presented himself to me early one morning while I was stationed at the front desk of the engineering department as secretary to the chief engineer. The young man was very upset and said, "I am a doctor and was just assigned here. I need immediate help with my office air conditioning. It is not working and my medical books will be ruined in this climate."

I responded, "Captain Anthony, I will certainly put you on the list. We have many on the list at this time with emergencies." I asked for his contact information. He mumbled and complained, stating he was a doctor and how could he be treated so badly. I was not the least impressed with his being a doctor, nor that he was very handsome.

I was focusing on my two-year contract, which was soon to come to an end, and investigating another two-year contract in Europe. Madrid or Spain was an option. I did not want any distractions. Captain Anthony left in a huff to another desk and made his request to them about his air conditioning. He was told he would have to go through Miss Verna. I was later told he asked a lot of questions about Miss Verna. Soon I was receiving flowers and invitations to the Officers' Club for dinner. I replied, "No thank you."

    He did get his air conditioning repaired but continued with his invitations to the Officers' Club. I relented and met him for dinner. He was a perfect gentleman and walked me to my car. He had his car shipped to the Canal Zone and I was invited to dinner in the Republic of Panama. He would drive. He seemed very concerned for my safety, and always was a gentleman. He spoke a lot about his first practice in a coal mining town. At dinner one night, he told me that he purchased a boat and would like to take me on a cruise. I had begun to trust him more and more, but I was hesitant because I couldn't swim! I had no access to pools or swim lessons when I was growing up.

Nevertheless, I accepted and was surprised that the boat had my name on it. After several months, he showed up with a very large diamond ring. It was too cumbersome for daily use. It was called a crown mount. I had never been impressed with jewelry. He asked me to marry him. He said, "If you marry me, I promise to take you to Europe too. I love you and want you to be my wife."

I was still very naive; I was soon to be 22 years old. He was a mature 27. I was impressed with his concern for my safety and well-being. I had come to trust him.

I trusted that he loved me. We girls at Notre Dame expected to save ourselves for a knight in shining armor, our Prince Charming. Anthony was respectful and a gentleman. I thought he fit the description of both. My answer was "Yes" to marrying him. The wedding was set at my family Catholic church in New Jersey. We both were able to arrange a short leave from the Army and traveled to New Jersey. After a short course on marriage at the church, we filled out and signed our individual marriage application, confirming that we were baptized and had never been married. Then it was off to get the marriage license. I chose a very simple gown at a bridal shop nearby. Before I left Panama I had a dressmaker make the two gowns for my sweet little sisters, Bianca and Emilia, who consented to be the bridesmaids. I was fortunate that my best friend at Notre Dame, Noreen, was available to be the maid of honor.

Before the wedding, I asked my mother for instruction on what to do on my wedding night. I had no idea. She said to ask my doctor husband. The four years at Notre Dame High, an all-girls school, had no sex education of any kind. When the senior prom was pending, the nuns required we bring our gowns to them to be approved for modesty. No strapless or low-cut gowns would be approved. They told us that if it was necessary to be traveling in one car with several couples, that we should bring a telephone book with us just in case we were forced to sit on our date's lap! I remember in my junior year at Notre Dame we were worried about sitting in the chair of a girl who became pregnant and had to be removed from Notre Dame in a hurry! Many of us believed we might get pregnant from sitting in her chair!

Hard to believe, but true. I told Anthony when he asked me to marry him that I had no experience with men. I don't think he understood the "no experience" as "none whatsoever." I asked him questions on the wedding night but he said not a word. I never came out of the bathroom at the hotel on my honeymoon night.

We returned to Panama and I was required to sign another two-year contract. I gave him my salary, as I thought a good wife should. Since we both joined the army as "single," we could not get housing.

We were forced to rent in the Republic. Anthony immediately put me on double doses of the first birth control pill. It had just been introduced and was later recalled. Anthony said he did not want me to get pregnant overseas. I heard no comment yet from the Church about birth control. Anthony decided that since he had a boat, that we should take up scuba diving. He received his certification immediately. He enrolled me for swim lessons and immediately after the swim class, enrolled me in scuba classes. I did well and passed the ocean test dive. He was off to purchase scuba gear. At that time there was only floating surface equipment, which supplied air with tube lines attached to a floating air supply on the surface. One could then plug in the floating supply to your gear. The drawback, he said, was that you could only dive to 40 feet. This was fine with me.

    I just wanted to discover God's creation underwater. I could see a lot while diving to 40 feet. I discovered the beautifully colored tropical fish and coral reefs. I was fascinated by God's creation. After Anthony saw the Thunderball movie, starring James Bond, self-contained tanks became available. He purchased the new gear for us. You were no longer restricted to 40 feet but were required to decompress slowly when returning to the surface. He also purchased the first self-contained underwater camera, the Nikonis. He said he wanted me to learn how to use it and I did.

    Anthony wanted me to take pictures of his friends shooting fish underwater at 80 feet using their bang sticks (or powerheads). (A 12-gauge shotgun shell attached to a diver's spear gun or pole could be aimed at the prey and then it would go off on contact.) The visibility was excellent and 300-pound groupers were prolific at 80 feet down. I was told that two to three divers would be required to aim at the grouper's head, shooting simultaneously to bring down the large fish. (Anthony said getting it on the boat would be another challenge). I was along to carry the gear and to take pictures of the hunt with the underwater camera. My first encounter was with a very friendly 300-pound grouper, which allowed me to pet him! As I was doing so and admiring the docility of this huge fish, more than twice my size, I noticed my husband and the other two divers taking aim to shoot him with their bang sticks. I immediately swam closer to the huge fish and placed myself directly in front of the grouper. The grouper was in no hurry to flee! I was treading water and motioning: DON'T SHOOT!

Anthony gave me the hand signal to return to the surface. I could see he was not happy. Arriving at the surface, treading water, he shouted, "What are you doing, embarrassing me in front of my friends!"

I answered back, "I don't think that the Grouper has a fair chance with those bang sticks. Why not use fishing poles?" (In Florida today, using bang sticks to hunt game fish is illegal. Bang sticks are only allowed in the state for diver protection.) Anthony and the divers continued their hunt without me and my pictures.

At the time, I had a 70-gallon saltwater tank and was studying ichthyology, the study of fish. Saltwater fish were so very interesting. I studied the colorful clown fish, who were so territorial, the baby octopus, and the male sea horses that carried the babies in their pouches. I had to take the baby sea horses out immediately after hatching and put them into another small saltwater tank to save them from being eaten. Then it was off to another trip with a new game plan! I was asked to take pictures of the divers shooting small fish; they left the dead fish on the ocean floor bottom with the intention to lure sharks out. They would then shoot the sharks and bring them topside on the boat.

I was then expected to take a "Trophy Picture." After the picture, they would use acid to remove the shark's teeth! The remains of the shark carcasses were thrown back into the ocean. Shark teeth jewelry was in then! This was way too much for me to witness, so I resigned as a photographer.

I told the divers that surely the Creator had a purpose for sharks, and it was not shark teeth jewelry. I told them it seemed like a Moby Dick event. I told them it just might come back to haunt them some day as it did Moby Dick. (Little did I know that years later it would come back to haunt me!)

After completing his tour of duty, and my own civilian contract, Anthony decided he would like to go to Jackson Memorial Hospital in Miami, Florida. He applied and was accepted for a residency in cardiology there. He sold both cars and purchased a new blue Mustang convertible from the Free Zone. I was told that my personal items (which could include his as well) would be shipped back to the United States at no charge, as per my civilian contract. I ordered some mahogany furniture to be built by manufacturers in the Republic. The prices were too good to pass up. These would be shipped at no charge as well.

The Army reminded me that I could get a refund from the four years I paid into my Army retirement fund. It was a large sum and I consented, thinking I would not be continuing working for the Army anytime soon.

The US Corps of Engineers announced that the section of the Pan-American Highway from Panama to Mexico was just completed. They stated that Mexico had contributed to the cost of this extension.

With this announcement came a warning from security that no one should drive at night. Bandits had been known to be active at night on this newly completed extension. The existing night lighting needed to be upgraded as well. There were no rest stops or gas stations yet. Anthony announced that we should drive the highway with the new car. He said we would drive during daylight as recommended, stopping at each country overnight. Then he would calculate how much fuel, water, and food we would need to arrive at the next overnight accommodation. Since his residency was approved in Miami, he said after driving through Mexico we would be able to proceed to the Army discharge station in Texas. As a civilian employee, I could skip the Texas discharge. I did not think this was a good idea since we could ship the car at no charge, fly to

Vera Marie Verna 41

the Texas discharge center, and then rent a car to Miami. The car and our belongings would be delivered once we gave the Army my new address. I thought it would be too long and dangerous driving in the daylight hours. Anthony said this would be a once in a lifetime adventure to drive the Pan-American Highway. He said, with no traffic on the highway, we would make good time. He said he would bring his gun with him and we would be safe. I relented and we were off immediately with supplies, which included gas containers, water, and an ice chest for food. He made the necessary calculations, staying overnight at sundown, and purchasing what we needed to get us to the next stretch. During the day there was absolutely no traffic at all on the new highway!

A few times we saw cattlemen driving their herds on the new highway. That was it. I found it necessary sometimes during the day to make a pit stop. There were no restrooms. Anthony was okay. I thought modesty demanded that I should walk a little off the highway to either side of the road. The sides of the highway were heavily secluded with large trees and bushes.

I did so and encountered a large animal with a long tail; it passed me so quickly that I could only see the back of it. I told Anthony I saw this animal and I thought it was a dog. Anthony said he did not think it was a dog. The highway was near mountains. He thought it was a mountain cat or cougar of sorts. That ended my rest stop routine fast!

I was enjoying the highway with its beautiful mountain views, gorgeous sunsets, and huge indigenous trees. Cactus trees of every sort lined either side of the highway. I could speak Spanish fluently, and quickly adapted to each country's slang version of Spanish. I was able to book the overnight accommodations, ask directions, and purchase supplies. Few spoke English.

As we drew closer to Mexico, the highway suddenly stopped!! A little more than 50 miles was not completed. Surprise! Surprise! Who to complain to about this critical error? Turning back was not an option. We drove ever so slowly during the day for those 50 miles and it took a week. This section was not only just dirt, but poorly cleared! It required the driver to be alert to navigate this obstacle course. The overnight accommodations, food, and gas were primitive and hard to find! I drove when Anthony needed a rest. I was surprised that he could sleep. I could not when he was driving. We finally completed those 50-plus miles and found access to the highway again. Now we encountered the highway going up and around the mountains of Mexico with narrow roads and no guard rails!!

We encountered a few trucks carrying cargo to Mexico. Anthony still thought this to be quite the adventure. No longer was I intrigued with the gorgeous, magnificent sunsets, or the abundant indigenous landscape on either side of the highway. For me it was a nightmare, especially when we could see below the cars and trucks that did not negotiate the mountainous hairpin turns without guard rails. We could see the wrecked cars and trucks below. I wondered what happened to those drivers? What adventure? What was so exciting about not having Triple A if you ran out of gas, or if your car was damaged and you needed a tow? The fact that we did not see one car compounded my thinking of all the what-ifs. Who could we flag down for assistance?

We finally arrived in Mexico. I was relieved but not for long. Seems like Montezuma's Revenge took over my body! Dr. Anthony was able to diagnose what it was. I was told not to eat their food!

It was a long haul to Texas to be discharged. I endured quietly and after his Texas discharge we were off to Miami, Florida. The little Mustang held up better than I did. I just lamented that it wasn't a jeep or something larger. Before I knew it, we purchased a small house in Coral Gables, quickly got a mortgage, and moved in. I notified the Army where to ship our personal items and furniture. Anthony was gone for long days and nights at Jackson Memorial. I decided to take classes at the University of Miami. I had so much time alone. I thought of pursuing a degree. I considered a teaching degree with a major in music. I found a reasonably priced old piano with ivory keys! Sister Rose Emilia from middle school had taught me well. A short Mozart piece was required for a concert for the final grade in music. My music professor said I would be required to play my piece without sheet music for the test. I had practiced only with sheet music. I told my professor that I could not do it without the sheet music. He suggested since I knew the piece so well with the sheet music to imagine the music resting on the piano; he told me to turn the pages and see the sheet music in my mind. So I practiced as he suggested. The morning of the exam I was the first student to be tested. I was ready early. Anthony said he could not make it to my concert and I was disappointed. I was stressed even though I was well prepared and practiced as I was instructed. When I arrived at the concert hall, there was only one concert piano on the stage and it was seated high above. Looking down onto the stage, there was seating for my professor, the other students, their instructors, and guests to support their student. The professor told me to take my place at the piano. I did and was shocked to find that there was no music rest for sheet music! The professor said to begin and to remember to see the sheet music in my mind's eye. As more people were arriving and filling the seating above me, I became nervous.

 I positioned my fingers on the keyboard telling myself that "I had this!" My hands started sweating profusely onto the keys. My fingers were frozen. The professor again said, "Begin!"

He announced that I was having trouble playing without sheet music. He said, "Play anything. Play some cords." I said a prayer but could play nothing! I failed the end of the year test and accepted that I would never become a music teacher or even a teacher, for that matter. I told Anthony I dropped out of the University of Miami and would sell the piano. We later moved to Fort Lauderdale. He completed his residency in cardiology, and was asked to stay on as a teaching professor at Jackson Memorial. I started college in Fort Lauderdale with a major in business, thinking I would have time on my hands again and would be able to study.

Boat named Vera Marie

Marriage to Dr. Anthony

CHAPTER 3

Walkers Cay/President Nixon/ Plane Crash

Anthony, still not in private practice, told me he had to take a second job at the close-by Fort Lauderdale Hospital as the evening physician for their emergency room. His hours were 8 p.m. to 5 a.m., five days a week, and he had to be on call for some weekends! He said he financed a 600-horsepower Donzi boat and a single engine Cessna aircraft. He said the down-payment check was short and it bounced. He told them to just add the difference to the aircraft loan! We had just financed the new Fort Lauderdale home with the proceeds from the Coral Gables home. I wondered if he used my retirement money toward the down payment for the boat and airplane. I don't think he ever checked his bank account. I took over the checking account.

I graduated from the Fort Lauderdale college with a major in business. I would now get a quick start with managing our business. I took over the house, airplane, and boat loans as well as insurance for all three. In addition to funding the airplane hangar as well as maintenance for the aircraft and the boat (the Fort Lauderdale house had a dock), there was gas for both to be budgeted. This was a challenge as the expenses took up most of his available income. Anthony asked me to start setting up trips from Fort Lauderdale Executive Airport to Walkers Cay, a small island off the coast of Miami owned by the Bahamian government. Any free time now was spent there. He was told about the wonderful visibility for scuba diving. His plan was to fly to Walkers Cay on weekends. Walkers Cay had a short landing strip on the island. For faster access, he would drive the boat over and leave it docked there and fly over to use the boat. (Another expense for the boat dockage.)

No more weekend duty for the emergency room. He continued with the week nights at the emergency room. One weekend we were introduced to President Richard Nixon and his friend Bebe Rebozo at Walkers Cay. Evidently, they were neighbors in Miami even before Nixon became president. They were relaxing by deep-sea fishing at the close-by island of Walkers Cay on Bebe Rebozo's boat. After Nixon became president, he and his friend would continue with this practice, but Nixon would fly by helicopter to the small island mostly on weekends.

We were having breakfast at the clubhouse when President Nixon came over to our table and asked Anthony if he would be interested in becoming the physician in residence at the island on weekends. Evidently the club manager told Nixon about our trips to Walkers Cay and that Anthony was a cardiologist at the Miami hospital. Nixon still maintained his home in Miami. He told Anthony that in return he would pay for dockage, all meals, and a villa available to stay in overnight. (We usually stayed on the boat overnight.) Anthony quickly said "Yes" and they shook hands.

No more weekend duty at the emergency room for Anthony. But he still worked week nights. Anthony then announced that he was setting up flying lessons for me. I had a few but was not at all interested in learning to fly. He said he hired a retired air force pilot as my instructor and would begin the following Saturday morning. Anthony would be bringing the boat over by himself and planned to meet us there after the lesson. I was up early Saturday and called the Executive Airport to have them take the airplane out of the hangar and put it on the runway. I asked that they be sure to top it off with gas. I arrived, met the instructor, and we were off to Walkers Cay. He entered first and myself second, as the only door was on my side. He was an older, heavy-set man. He took off flying with one hand on the controls.

He talked a lot and was confident that I could take over the controls. I did, but as we were approaching for landing, he took back the controls. He had never landed at this short, private landing strip. I mentioned to him that I had landed there many times, and that he was coming in too low on his approach to the landing strip. He did not make the correction! The landing gear collapsed when it hit the edge of the runway. (We were not high enough to make contact with the landing strip. He had come in too low!) The plane bounced up from the hard hit when the landing gear made contact with the side wall of the runway. Fortunately when it bounced up, it slammed back down onto the runway and not the ocean! I don't know if I would be around to recount this event if it had slammed into the ocean. There is no explanation whatsoever of why it bounced up, bringing the aircraft in contact with the landing strip instead of the ocean. The aircraft now had no landing gear or wheels, since the landing gear had collapsed under the aircraft. With no wheels or any part of the landing gear, sliding from one side of the runway to the other on its belly, destroying what was left of the aircraft, it came to an abrupt stop.

The instructor then announced that he was going to the clubhouse to call a helicopter to pick him up right away because the Bahamian authorities would require a large fine for crashing on their territory. He said he might even lose his license. He then proceeded to climb over me as this was the only door out. He had to kick the door open because it was damaged. He was so heavy I could hardly breathe.

When out, he started running up the hill to the clubhouse. I was in shock. I got out and looked at the damage. It was in complete ruin. I thought to try to salvage some of the equipment, but I remembered that I had just ordered it to be topped off with gas. I thought it could have exploded and it was still possible that it could explode any time. I did not attempt to salvage anything and was so very thankful that the aircraft did not fall back to the ocean. I could not imagine the pilot trying to kick the damaged door open under water! I got out and stood there for a long time, staring at the damaged aircraft. I knew I was in shock, but I wondered how I was still able to function. I said to myself that this was not a piano recital gone wrong! Maybe I would be able to face other disasters in my life after this one and not panic. As I was standing there, the club manager came down the hill from the clubhouse on a golf cart. He said, "You need to get this aircraft off the runway!" He did not ask if I was okay. He repeated again, "Get this aircraft off the runway!" (President Nixon sometimes arrived by helicopter.)

I don't know how I found the composure to reply, "If you want to remove what's left of this aircraft, go right ahead and do it! However, do be careful— it was just topped off with gas. It might explode at any time." He just stared as I calmly walked up the hill to the clubhouse and took a seat on a sofa. I lost track of time when someone approached me and said, "Your husband arrived by boat and went to check out his aircraft." (To check out his aircraft before checking out his wife!) Later he came over to me saying, "The aircraft is completely totaled. You will have to call the insurance company."

Anthony said, "We will fly back by helicopter to the Fort Lauderdale Executive Airport where you left the car." I told him I cannot fly back. I told him I didn't think I could fly again. I was so emphatic that he said, "Okay, we will take the boat back." Years thereafter, I could not fly even commercial. When I would hear the landing gear go down, I would relive the crash landing every time. I decided to order a flying lesson. I called the airport and asked for an appointment for a lesson with a certified instructor and their aircraft. After landing, the instructor said, "When do you want to schedule your next lesson?" I said, "Never!" I told her the reason why and she said, "Well you needed to get right back up after the crash landing." I should of, could of, but I did not. I was thankful that finally I was free from that nightmare.

Anthony was hardly ever around between Walkers Cay and his two jobs. I had heard of the Merry Widows' Club for Fort Lauderdale doctors' wives. I was told by Anthony to be home by 7:30 p.m.

He said he would worry too much unless I was home by 7:30 p.m. I was to find out later the true reason for this restriction. I thought the Merry Widows' Club would give me an opportunity to be around doctors' wives. Maybe they could suggest how to survive so much time alone. Maybe I could receive some council from them. I found out I was the youngest member. Anthony said "okay" reluctantly. I immediately called to join and make arrangements for their next night out. I thought we would be going to the theater, a musical event, or just out to dinner. I could have conversations and just get to know some of them. I soon found out why they were called the Merry

Widows! The only outings were to bars, high-dollar bar lounges, and mostly just bars! Not only could I not have a conversation with them, but they were so tipsy that I could not understand a word they were saying! I realized that I was not good with alcohol. Half a glass of wine or champagne or even beer had to be mixed with water and be on ice. There was no way to able to keep up with them. Even if I could, how would I be able to understand what they were saying? I resigned from the club and told Anthony that I would have to pursue other options. He said there were no other options. I could not believe what he then suggested! He said we should book a three week trip to Europe.

"I promised I would take you to Europe and we will stop in Madrid." I agreed immediately, thinking I might be able to repair the separation anxiety I was experiencing for so long in our marriage as well as satisfying my dream to explore Europe. He said he was leaving for California to visit his cousin who was a well-known plastic surgeon. He said he had not seen him in quite a while. When he arrived home after four days, he announced that he could not go with me to Europe. I told him I had booked the trip but it could be changed to another time and not to worry. He said, "No. I cannot go with you so why not ask your mother if she wants to take over my ticket?" He continued, "There is still time to do that." He then made a comment, looking straight at me with a serious look and tone. "You still have the innocent face of an angel. So innocent!" I did not know what that meant. I thought, *so innocent?* I was comforted that he communicated something! I called my mother who immediately agreed to take over Anthony's ticket.

CHAPTER 4

Promised Trip to Europe

Mom and I began our trip in Portugal. Mom seemed happy to travel but was not big on the walking tours. We went to the prominent sites, historic churches, and famous restaurants. I would have preferred to mingle more with the locals and dine with them. Next stop: Spain. I had investigated with the University of Pennsylvania about their archaeological expeditions before I left. I learned that there were two active digs. One in old Carthage and the other on the island of Crete. I told mom we could take a bus trip. She was not interested but we did get on the bus that would take us to Carthage. She said it was too hot, there were too many flies, and there were no restaurants.

We turned around and came back. I then told her we would go to the wonderful historic air conditioned museum in downtown Madrid. She consented to the museum and to the hair and nail appointments I had set up for her at a salon nearby. I decided to have my hair cut shorter for easier maintenance while traveling. She was happy with the works!

We then proceeded to lunch and off to the museum. The museum had high ceilings, very wide showrooms with lots of historical paintings and historical items on each side. The museum assistants offered guided tours but you could take your time with a large chart-like guide book that had explanations in English for each item and their significant details. I thought I would like the "do it yourself tour" because I could take time to read aloud each explanation to mom.

I read aloud each item. It was so very detailed and interesting. I was absorbed in describing each item.

We finished the left side of the first showroom. I looked over to my left to tell mom that we would continue to the other side. There was no mom! Another woman had been following me down the aisle listening to my explanations of each item. I turned and looked back to the beginning of the tour and there was mom sitting on a bench provided for those waiting to begin a tour. I walked back and asked Mom, "What happened?" I told her I did not realize it was not her. I was reading aloud and was so absorbed that I didn't realize another woman was following me. Mom said her feet were really hurting and she would try to buy other shoes. She wanted to go back to the hotel.

Next stop: Italy. I did get her some new shoes, but to no avail, as they needed to be broken in and that did not solve the issue. A priest in Philadelphia had arranged for us to join a small group that would be addressed by Pope Paul VI. A tour of the Vatican would follow. I was excited to tour the Sistine Chapel. I brought books on Michelangelo's work. I wanted to see them all. The famous *Pieta*, *Mother and Child* in Florence, and the *David*. The leaning tower of Pisa and so many other sites were a must see. Mom said she could not go any further after attending the audience with the pope. She said she wanted to go home! I tried to talk her out of it, but no luck. I took her to the airport, and asked that she bring my luggage back as well. I was determined to continue on with one small carry-on shoulder bag. I helped mom pack, brought her to the airport, and waited for her to board the aircraft. Now I could continue without luggage so I didn't have to wait for a porter to check me in or out at airports or hotels.

I had purchased the Arthur Frommer book *Europe on Five Dollars a Day* before I left Florida. It served me well for the rest of the trip and I stayed at recommended hostels. I found the accommodations clean and they were located in the safest locations. I enjoyed the recommended tour sites and dining at the recommended cafes rather than the fancy restaurants. I went back to the Vatican to finish the tour and spent a lot of time in Rome. I visited the Leaning Tower of Pisa and the amazing town of Venice, before taking the train to Florence. My room had a view of the Arno River with antique furniture and even an antique poster bed which was clean and convenient. I could walk to Michelangelo's *Pieta* and *David*. Thank you Arthur Frommer!

    I stayed for a week. There were free outdoor concerts every night, some indoor concerts, and operas. I attended as many as I could. The *Pieta* and the *David* were magnificent. I sat in front of both for a day, admiring them. I was able to see the *Pieta* before it was later vandalized. Many young people frequented the outdoor free concerts, which were mostly classical music. I counted myself fortunate that most of them spoke English very well. They were going to school in Italy and spoke Italian as well. There were some from the United States but most were from Europe. They were quick to share and to recommend small, friendly cafes. The food was excellent and the diners friendly. I stayed so long in Florence that I decided to skip the trip to France.

I wanted to see more of Greece and England. My mother advised Anthony that I would keep to my schedule and would arrive back to Fort Lauderdale with the same flight information that was on his copy of my ticket.

I sent Anthony many postcards from each country I visited. When sending him the postcards from Italy (he was Italian), I wrote that I found him to be more handsome than all the Italian men in Italy and that I could not wait to recount all the details of the trip. Now I was off to Athens, Greece. While I was walking the Parthenon, I met two French airline stewardesses. They spoke excellent English and told me they were headed to Crete, their favorite stop after Athens. They said they made the trip every year and asked me if I would like to come along. I would be able to stay at their favorite place in Crete. I quickly answered yes! (Even though I heard that there were some military clashes occurring with protests from Greek revolutionaries.)

    I quickly returned to my hostel, checked out, and met them at the airport in Athens. The ticket did not cost much since it was a very short flight from Athens to Crete. The French stewardesses also spoke Greek and helped me with the issues before boarding in Athens and when we arrived at the Crete airport. The Crete accommodations were very clean and located downtown. The five dollars a day plan included a great breakfast. We went to dinner at their favorite Greek restaurant. I told them I would be leaving early in the morning to check out the archaeological dig on top of the mountain. I told them the last bus left at 5 p.m. and I would be sure to meet them for dinner. There was only one bus leaving to travel to the top of the mountain. On my short walk to the bus, I saw many Greek Orthodox priests in their black garb with hats and beards. When the bus stopped, I went into the small cafe there. Older Greeks were sitting outside. I inquired about how to get to the dig. I was told to stay on the narrow road just out front. It went to the top.

I had brought along a little book describing what was going on at the dig and began the walk. It spoke about what was to be encountered. Centuries of ancient civilizations at every level of the dig were to be so very carefully uncovered by the archaeologists. The views from the narrow road were magnificent. On either side I could see farmers picking their produce and tending their fields. There were many who were herding goats on the narrow road. One older Greek woman on the left side of the road was harvesting tomatoes.

She motioned to me and we had a wonderful "sign language conversation." She motioned if I would like a large tomato that she just picked. I nodded yes and she handed it to me, smiling. I proceeded to take a bite. She asked, pointing to my ring finger, if I was married. I responded yes. Then she made a rocking motion with her arms like she was holding a baby to ask if I had any children. I responded and shook my head no. She smiled and laughed at lot. I thought what a great friendly conversation we had without words! She smiled and I waved goodbye as I continued on my way to the dig. I saw colorfully dressed Gypsies on their horses, which were also outfitted with colorful blankets and carried produce that was stacked and wrapped on either side. What a scene. They tipped their hats and smiled. I thought I was watching a National Geographic movie. What friendly people!

As I neared the top of the mountain, I noted the locations they were working on. There were some reports under glass with explanations of their findings, but there was no office or anyone around to speak with. I stayed for a long time looking at everything and would have to wait until I returned home to call the university to ask more questions. At least I brought my book on the Crete expedition and could read it again and again on what they expected to find. Even the Trojan Horse event was cited.

I continued back down, as I did not want to miss the last bus, and encountered more Gypsies and farmers bringing their harvest down the road. I was on time for dinner with the French stewardesses and recounted what I saw. They introduced me to orzo, the local wine, which I tasted and then diluted. I had never been much for wine. I preferred dry champagne diluted half and half, because even diluted it was bubbly. They introduced me to the Greek version of a hot dog. It consisted of baked lamb wrapped on a stick.

It was better than a hot dog. I was told it was just baked without any nitrates or preservatives. My two French friends were heading back to the airport the next morning after breakfast. I planned to leave as well with them. It was a very sad goodbye for me. I was sorry I could not fit in my trip to France. My encounter with the French was so very memorable and gave me a new appreciation for them as well as the Greeks. I was now off to London, England. I noted the buses, cabs, and cars driving on the left side of the road. I got used to it since I used the buses to go everywhere. I checked into a very clean hostel downtown. The location was great for walking tours. The British were so very polite and helped with directions and how to calculate converting my US dollars. First stop was their fabulous museum. It had every countries' treasures that I was not able to visit: the Egyptian mummies, the oldest bibles, and the original famous paintings and artifacts from many countries, including Israel.

One afternoon, I decided to walk over to Hyde Park. Two boys approached me and began a conversation. When I turned and spoke to them, they became angry, for they thought I was a young boy. No makeup, short hair, and I was walking in the park alone dressed in pants and Dingo boots. I can understand their disappointment.

I was not interested in the local restaurants. I noticed that the food I was expecting to be cold was hot. What I expected to be hot was cold, like the porridge soups. I visited Harrods department store, which was the biggest and the most well-known at the time. They had everything one could imagine at Harrods, but with high prices.

Nevertheless, it was a must see. I was interested in the British Parliament and found it. I was able to sit in on some of their debates, which were open to the public. The delivery of those speakers and their accents debating with such enthusiasm so very politely was fascinating.

The Big Ben clock impressed me too. I would have liked to investigate the countryside, but I wanted to return on time according to my flight and arrival date back to Fort Lauderdale. I arrived on time.

I waited, but no Anthony. There were no cell phones back then, but I tried our landline and his hospital phone number, but no answer. I waited for quite a while and then decided to take a cab to the house. When I arrived, the only car in front was the Jaguar XKE, which Anthony said he had purchased for me.

He purchased an orange Corvette for himself. I could hardly see over the steering wheel of the Jaguar. It was low to the ground and uncomfortable. I could feel every bump. At the stop signs and red lights, guys would roll down their window after revving up their engines and ask if I wanted to race. I would never have chosen this car because it was a stick shift and it was not blue! I had the house key and went in.

CHAPTER 5

The Surprise Divorce/ Disconnect from God

The house was cleaned out! I thought someone robbed the house. I found my things on the second-floor bedroom. All the furniture was gone, even in Anthony's office as well as his clothing. I walked outside and the boat was gone. While I was standing there, my neighbor, Mary, who had befriended me so many times, had lost their little two-year-old boy. Her husband, not knowing the little one was behind his car, ran over him and he died. This happened before I moved in and they told me what a horrible mourning process they went through. They told me the way they were able to get through was because of their faith in God. They had become mature Christians and were so kind and always ready to help. Mary said that my mother- and father-in-law brought a moving van about a week ago and moved everything out. She said she did not see Anthony's Corvette since I left for my trip. She and her husband were shocked. She told me that if there was anything I needed, I could come over. I went inside and tried to call every phone number I could to get hold of Anthony, including his parents' phone number.

    I finally fell asleep on some blankets. The next morning, Anthony called to tell me his parents were going to be serving me divorce papers and had hired an attorney to sue for divorce. He told me that they said I was a liability because he accepted an offer to join a prestigious cardiology practice. His parents said I would not fit in as I had no degree or profession.

    He told me that when he was in medical school he had gotten a nurse pregnant. He married her but his parents wanted him to divorce, insisting she and the baby were a liability to his career. They would not allow them to visit them with the child, and they hired a lawyer to divorce her too. The nurse then married another man and would accept no support from Anthony nor grant him permission to ever see his daughter. He would go to the day-care center where he was to try to get a glimpse of her. He said that was why he asked the gynecologist to perform every fertility test available at the time for infertility. The gynecologist said he could find nothing wrong with me. He said it could have been the double doses of the first birth control pill.

I did remember the gynecologist pinpointing my time of ovulation. He started a procedure whereby I would take Anthony's sperm in a container and, with the container under my arm (the doctor said to keep it warm), I proceeded to the gynecologist's office where I would be inseminated with his sperm. This went on for six months with no luck and was discontinued.

Anthony said he would call my priest and tell him he was married before, had a child, and divorced the mother. He would tell him he lied on the marriage application. The marriage would be annulled and I could remarry! I replied and asked him how he could go along so easily with his parents then and now? No reply! I became very lightheaded and thought I should sit down, but there were no chairs. It took me more than a few days to call anyone or even recount this to Mary and her husband.

He did call my priest and the priest said that the marriage could probably be annulled but that he was very concerned for me now. When I finally told Mary, she said, "Persevere! You can get through this." I told her I did not believe in divorce and would not consent to a divorce. She agreed. I was served the divorce papers. My gynecologist and his wife heard about the pending divorce and befriended me. They told me everyone knew that Anthony was consorting with the nurses at the emergency room. Everyone knew about it but me. They told me to call their high-dollar attorney. They said not to worry about paying the attorney as Anthony would have to pay his fee no matter who won.

Grievous fault would have to be proven against me. The gynecologist's wife called me and reassured me that I would be able to get the house, the car, and hefty monthly payments for support. She said, "If you want to divorce him, wait until he is in practice for a long time, but in the meantime call the lawyer." I called the lawyer and he confirmed that the divorce would be impossible; I would get hefty monthly payments for support and he would not be granted a divorce because there was no sign of a no-fault divorce law in progress. When I recounted all this to Mary, she said, "Great, you can stay in the house and get the support without divorcing." She did not believe in divorce either. A week or so later, Mary showed up with an advertisement that was in a Fort Lauderdale newspaper.

The advertisement said a family was looking for a Nannie who could speak Spanish, for two children. The ad stated that the Nannie would be required only when they traveled. Mary said, "You are perfect for the job! It would be a good distraction for you and help you get through this trial."

I called the number and set up an appointment, which was at a high-dollar restaurant in Fort Lauderdale. I arrived, but only the husband showed up. He asked me for my credentials and I gave him my resume. He asked me more questions, and we ordered food.

The man started talking to me in Spanish and asked more questions. That is the last thing I remembered! I was going to ask where he lived and how much to expect from each trip. I also wanted to know the children's ages. I remembered nothing. I woke up in the morning alone, half dressed in a motel room. I had been raped. I don't know how my car got from the restaurant to the motel. My keys were in my purse. In a daze, I proceeded to the house. I was so angry, convicting myself, thinking how could I have been so naive and stupid! Did I not know that there is more evil in the world than I could ever imagine? Why wasn't I more careful?! I felt so much shame and intense conviction. I could not talk to anyone including the police! Shame and regret were rampant whether I was awake or asleep. Nightmares that I could have been raped by more than one person haunted me. Who drove my car to the motel? I shouted out, "Where were you God?!" The surprise divorce with Anthony's disclosures would have been enough to destroy me. I had tried to be a good wife even though it was difficult.

My anger took over. I could not speak to Mary. When she asked me how it went with the interview, I changed the subject. I was angry with her too for showing me the advertisement. I was more angry with God. I questioned my own identity. Who am I? Certainly I am not the same person anymore. I recall angry words. "I don't need you, God. I don't need Anthony either. I will make it on my own. I don't want help from anyone! I will give Anthony his divorce. Who cares. Give it to him!" I called the attorney and asked him when the hearing was and to accelerate it. I did not tell the attorney that I would give him the divorce! The morning of the hearing at the court house I drove there alone and when I entered, Anthony and his parents were sitting together. They motioned me to pick up the wedding album that they had taken from the house when they cleaned it out! I paid no attention and refused it. My attorney was sitting with me and joking, telling me, "You will get everything! We will easily win!" He said they have such a weak case. Anthony's lawyer presented their case. He stated that I was overbearing, bothering him about the dangers of his sky diving, and embarrassing him in front of his friends.

He alleged that I was no longer interested in his activities. I listened quietly without any expression, as I knew what I was going to do.

The judge heard from my attorney who presented my case and asked for everything short of a divorce.

The judge asked me to come forward to speak. The judge said if ever he had presented a case to his wife for divorce like this one, she would have pushed him out of the fifth floor window of this court house. I stood up, and to the horror of my attorney said, "Your Honor, go ahead and give him his divorce! I want nothing from him at all. Not his money, the Jaguar, or the house. I don't even want his name! I do want a $50,000 life insurance policy to cover the earned money I gave him these past seven years. I will vacate the house in six months and leave the car."

My attorney was furious! The judge granted the divorce. I abruptly left the room with my attorney following me down the elevator and screaming, "What have you done! You are being so altruistic! You will regret this."

I responded, "What is your problem? You will get paid your large fee from Anthony."

I never looked back. I decided to apply for a job on Galt Ocean Mile, a well-to-do area in Fort Lauderdale near the house. I got the job. I was to be secretary to the owner-broker of a well-known real estate office on Galt Ocean Mile. I would write contracts, answer the phones for the listing agents, and type their sales contracts. I was always the last to leave for the day. I quickly got the hang of the business and wanted to sit for my real estate license. I looked much younger than 27 so I purchased clear glasses to appear older and more experienced. I now had money, so I also purchased a car after six months. It was a used blue Volvo station wagon. This would be okay for hauling and transporting clients.

I also enrolled at the House of Albert Modeling School near Galt Ocean Mile. I quickly finished the course and was paid to model high-dollar clothes for teas, lunches, and other functions on Galt Ocean Mile. I was given leave by my employer for the events and modeling engagements, as they were near the office. The best part was that I got to keep the clothes after the events! I thought this would be good as it was appropriate to "dress for success" at this job. I was convinced I did not need God, the church, or anyone for that matter. Since I was on salary, I looked for a rental after six months. It was small but well located.

CHAPTER 6

Second Marriage/Anthony's Disappearance

While I was still living at the Fort Lauderdale house, a patient of my gynecologist and his wife called me. They were the ones who recommended the attorney. They made me aware of what everyone knew about Anthony's affairs. They also told me that one of the nurses was pregnant with Anthony's child. My friends thought that this woman, Jackie, who was a friend of my gynecologist's wife, would be a good contact for me. She said Jackie was very Catholic, but that did not interest me at all.

I was no longer practicing any religion. Jackie called me and was very bubbly and intelligent about business issues. She ran her husband's business for years. We were the same age. I spent a lot of sleepovers at her home with late night conversations about my life with Anthony. At one point, she brought me over to the home of a Polish family who had been friends of hers and her mother for years.

I was introduced to the Polish family and also to their son, Thomas. He had just returned from Vietnam. The family was concerned that he had post-traumatic stress disorder. I met with the family several times because they were most hospitable. They asked me if I wanted to accompany the family to their Catholic church. I declined without any explanation. Thomas seemed very upbeat and friendly, as was the rest of his large family. He said he was going to college to become a CPA. He did not live at their house but at a local funeral parlor! He was allowed to stay there rent free and helped the director with organizing funerals. I thought, "Well, to each his own!" I continued with my long hours of work, seeing him off and on.

He invited me to dinner one day and he shared some of what he was dealing with. I shared some of my story. He said the wonders of the heavens had helped him. He said I should try looking up at the sky. We tried it together and it did help looking at the night sky. The silence and the clear night with the moon and the stars was very calming and peaceful. He shared that he needed to write an essay in order to graduate in accounting. He said it was too much for him and asked if I had any suggestions. I told him I would help write his required essay. I did. He received an "A" on his assignment and graduated. When I saw him weeks later, he was smiling. I don't know how or why, but I was able to see a glimpse of a suffering man.

I had so much going on and no time to give it much thought. Thomas had asked me to live with him. I thought, "Why not?" He moved into my small apartment. His Catholic family was not pleased.

Some months later, I heard on the radio and television news about a well-known physician who had disappeared after taking off from the Fort Lauderdale Executive Airport in a twin-engine aircraft. I surmised it was the replacement for his single engine that was totaled. The report said that he did not file a flight plan and that they had no idea where to search for him. The report said that they did receive a Mayday call from an aircraft, but since he did not file a flight plan, it was of no help. They searched the immediate area, but after two weeks the search was called off. Some thought he might have flown into the Bermuda Triangle, since some reports of disappearing aircraft were thought to have flown there. As the news reports continued, the *Miami Herald* reported that a psychic who had assisted the Miami Police on other missing person cases notified the *Herald* that the doctor's airplane had crashed somewhere off the coast in shallow water. She said that he was injured and in danger of being eaten by sharks! She told them not to discontinue the search but to escalate it. The news reported that it was extended for another week with a search party of helicopters. It was then reported that the search was called off at the end of the week because nothing was found; no wreckage and no body!

 For months I had nightmares about his whereabouts. I thought maybe it was staged, but that did not make sense since he was finally in practice. I was told years later that he could have been with the CIA. A retired Army soldier that was a friend of mine had connections with a general and the Pentagon. When asked for access to Anthony's file, he was told to keep his nose out of it!

He said they preceded that order with some very unsavory language. My friend told me it was a top security file. Well this upset me even more. Knowing Anthony was a fan of James Bond and his cousin was a leading plastic surgeon in California (he met him before I left for my trip to Europe), this introduced a whole new set of scenarios to ponder! Maybe I should contact the Army.

I told my friend about what I was thinking. He said: YOU DON'T MESS WITH THE CIA! My reaction was not to give up. It was a similar feeling to those wives and relatives that were told their son or husband was lost in action. They did not know if he was dead or alive or in a prisoner of war camp. I found myself thinking similar to those relatives of POWs lost in action. I had several nightmares that he was alive and that I could find him myself. In my dream I would see him alone on a boat. I would ask, "What happened to you? Where are you—are you okay?"

If someone looked like him from a distance or if I heard a voice that sounded like his, I would follow the man to see if it was Anthony. Other nightmares included the Moby Dick advice I gave to Anthony and the other divers. I told them that killing sharks for their teeth might come back to haunt them as it did Moby Dick. It continued to be a "haunting experience" for me.

I was still living with Thomas and working hard after securing my real estate sales and broker's license. I was hired by a commercial realty group to manage their west office.

I managed to sell a commercial piece of real estate myself. Money was no issue. I purchased a small house and we moved from my rental. Thomas' family continued to be upset with us, but I continued to work hard and was always the last to leave the office. About a year later, I decided to purchase a charming old house one block off the ocean. The sellers had owned it for a while. It needed a lot of renovations. The mortgage payment was affordable. I thought to rent or sell my small house. I was collecting commissions now on my own purchases, rentals, and sales.

I thought I should install my real estate office in the building. I incorporated and did so. I started investigating the renovations. The electric was so outdated. The wiring was exposed without casing and there was no insulation. I found very old newspapers between the original stucco and exterior walls.

There were huge oak trees on the oversized property. I wanted to know more of this charming old building.

It had a magnificent original barrel-tile roof and Key West wood floors in good condition. The front reception room was very large and had a coral rock fireplace that needed some careful reconditioning. It was the original. The living room was magnificent, with 16-foot french doors across the entire front wall, providing great lighting to the interior. The historical society was just a few blocks away. I made an appointment to find out more about this charming building that was one block away from the ocean. It was a good thing I did not start renovations. I was told it was the oldest building in Boca Raton! The society was happy as well that I came to see them.

They said they wanted to assist me with the renovations to preserve its history. They offered me history books on early Boca Raton and lots of pictures, which I devoured. They confirmed that the building was built by the first major of Boca Raton, himself a realtor. They asked if I would like to meet his daughter, Diane, who was writing a book on the history of Boca Raton. The daughter was now up in age and had retired just a few blocks away. Her father called the house Morada Bonita.

At the time, he owned an adjoining acreage and sold trees of every kind. He sold the acreage years later. It was called the Palmetto Plantation. The road to the ocean was named Palmetto Park Road. I enjoyed being with Diane. She told me lots of stories about the history of the house and her family. Her mother bought and sold antiques at her own antique shop downtown. Diane gave me a few of her mother's antiques, which I still treasure. The second floor was a large bedroom with lots of windows to catch the ocean breezes. She said the 35 years she lived at the house, it was never damaged by a single hurricane. She said there were more issues from pirates who would come ashore from the ocean!

I incorporated, set up my office, and was soon earning a minimum of $150,000 a year. I purchased several other rental properties with some on the Intercoastal Waterway and within a few years my net worth was over two million. I continued for ten years at this location with my real estate business.

I discovered that Thomas had a gambling and drinking problem to such an extent that I would get calls from the police for his drunk driving and had to go to bail him out. In another incident, he totaled his car. He was glad no one was injured or he would have gone to jail for drunk driving.

I found out he was taking money out of our joint account to buy stocks and to gamble at local card games, even though gambling was not yet legal in the state of Florida.

I tried to get away with him often with trips to the Florida Keys and on cruises. I thought this would help. On one cruise, I never got to see him at all since gambling was permitted back then but only on cruise ships. It was not legal yet in Florida. He was busy gambling and drinking nonstop.

He lost all of his money. He did not even have enough to pay the small, required docking charge that was due when the cruise ship docked. He had resigned from his accounting years earlier and did not want to be a CPA. He said he wanted to work with his hands. A friend who had been with him in Vietnam was a CPA himself. He told me that Thomas was drinking a lot and using drugs during the war. He talked to him about joining his firm, but Thomas was not interested. This went on for three more years. When I would try to talk to him about it, he would start joking with me about every situation. He gave no clue as to what he was dealing with. He said I never went to church with him and he had stopped going himself because I did not marry him in the church, and this was the problem. I agreed to marry him in the church. His family and friends of his family were delighted!

In the meantime, I called a local gynecologist. I wanted to know about my fertility. We had not used any type of birth control. The doctor ordered a procedure to see if my tubes were blocked. Everything was okay. He could find no reason why I could not get pregnant. Thomas refused to be tested.

I thought I would ask Thomas if he wanted to adopt after seven years with no children. He said absolutely not! I had asked Anthony the same question and his answer was the same. I was surprised with Thomas' answer as he came from a large family.

I proceeded to set up the marriage ceremony at a local Catholic church that his family favored. The wedding date was set. They were so happy and invited their family and friends. There was to be an after party—very simple and catered. My two brothers were there. My little brother, Patrick, who was a very good photographer, offered to take pictures. We arrived at the church and the ceremony began.

I was asked, "Do you take this man..."

I said, "I do."

The priest asked Thomas the same question and he did not answer—but fainted! They held him up and asked him the same question. He fainted again. The third time, they called an ambulance and took him out of the church on a stretcher. Patrick was snapping pictures like crazy. I stood there looking down on the stretcher with the paramedics who were saying that they were sorry to ruin my honeymoon.

They said he should be taken to the hospital. All his vital signs were okay, but that he should go to the hospital, as they did not know what was wrong.

I was standing near the priest and I asked him if we should reschedule. The priest said, "No. You are okay to go," and gave me the church marriage certificate. We had already applied for the civil marriage certificate. I was okay with just that. Then Thomas did not want to go with the paramedics to the hospital and suddenly felt well enough to go to the reception!

I was still not practicing any religion. I was not concerned, but his family was hysterical! Three more years and I had enough. It was ten years of trying to make the marriage work. I called my attorney friend and told him to give Thomas half of everything and to do a speedy one. He asked, "Are you sure you want to give him half?" and I replied, "Yes, just do it."

Thomas moved into one of the intercoastal townhouse properties. A year later he said he felt guilty and gave it back to me. I was sleeping upstairs in the building. He moved to another one and rented what was left. I would see him a lot more often than when we were together. He was still drinking a lot with his friends at his own condominium. One young builder gave him work and was staying with Thomas because he had just been divorced as well. He was a heavy drinker and died from alcoholism soon after moving in with Thomas. Thomas said he wanted to stop drinking when he witnessed his friend dying, but did not go to Alcoholics Anonymous or seek help.

    I was now converting the building to a restaurant and art gallery with art gifted by the historical society. They helped me again with the restaurant renovations. I installed a separate French door entrance to a large room that was adjoining the building for the realty business. I was glad to not have to relocate the business, as the address had been the same for the last ten years. The restaurant was now a go with the real estate business.

    The large reception room with the fireplace was perfect for the diners to sit while waiting for a table. It was reservations only. The historical society gifted me with many old photos.

    The restaurant was a perfect addition to the art gallery. The dining rooms were furnished with antique reproduction furniture ordered from Georgia. I chose reproduction dishes and glasses and received a license to serve wine and beer. I asked my New York chef from Tavern on the Green in New York to prepare food that was common in the 1920s era. The historical society gave me some old cookbooks and the chef was able to use them for the menu.

    The first luncheon was to be in honor of the historical society! They all came to sample the new dishes, furniture, and antique shop. Most of all, they enjoyed sampling the "antique food" that was served. My friend Diane showed up as well. Now I was inviting the leading developers and builders to lunch at the Morada Cafe. At times it was more convenient to take them to the Boca Raton hotel and club for lunch. The hotel offered more variety with their menu. Diane, my friend, was also invited to lunches at the Morada Cafe and Boca hotel. Sometimes heads of state who were visiting the Boca hotel liked reserving the entire building for their dinners, preferring the smaller building over the large hotel, for security reasons. Weddings were performed at the charming building sometimes, with lunch to follow.

    Many years later, after my born-again experience, I was told by a Catholic priest that I should apply for an annulment for the marriage to Thomas while there were still witnesses around. My brother Patrick's pictures of Thomas fainting were still available but not needed.

They found the priest who performed the wedding. He was in retirement. He confirmed the marriage was never completed and was severely reprimanded. After speaking with Thomas as well, within a week the marriage of ten years was annulled! That would make a total 17 years of marriages annulled. There were no children during those 17 years and no birth control of any kind was used.

Patrick came to visit me after the second divorce and was so concerned, saying that I looked like a different person. He said I looked depressed. We would have meals together at the restaurant. He liked concerts and musicals. His condo was just around the comer. I helped him purchase a small condominium. We furnished it and I would rent it out seasonally. He would visit me off season. We were able to spend time together. He was editor for a small newspaper in North Florida. One day he showed up with a press pass for us to attend a luncheon at the country club for a popular newscaster.

He was the youngest of six. He was always concerned about his big sister and the many disappointments that he was able to witness in my life. A few years later on one of his visits, he told me he had contracted AIDS. He said I was the only one he could talk to about it.

Antiques and food meet

By Ellie Lingner
Special to The News

Tucked at the east foot of the Intracoastal bridge on the north side of Palmetto Park Road in Boca Raton is a diminutive beige stucco house with round brown awnings.

Built in the early part of the century by Boca Raton pioneer Harley Gates, the building currently is home to Vera Verna, her dog, her real estate business and her restaurant, the Morada Cafe.

The tiny cafe seats only 20 and the atmosphere is a blend of antique and informal. You want a menu? Just ask. It changes every day. "We serve what is available and fresh," says Verna.

You can't eat salt? Just tell chef Scoti Sabatino. Your meal will be salt free. Sabatino has worked at Michael's Palm Cafe in Town Center and the Governor's Club in Palm Beach. But cooking to order and using whole, fresh foods with no shortcuts is the kind of thing you can do only in such a tiny restaurant, he says.

Sabatino whips up unusual dishes like salmon with wasabi in sesame and soy; veal with fresh tomato, basil and baby artichoke hearts; and scallops sauteed in fennel, garlic and pernod.

Working at the Morada Cafe allows Sabatino to stretch his creative limits. He likes that. So does Verna. Her specialty is also creativity, whether in development of a real estate project like Charleston Place, a replica of the old south, or a restaurant where the decorative focal points are a 1925 Zenith floor model radio and a coral stone fireplace.

DISTINCTIVE DINING

Verna spotted the building that was to be her future home in 1977. She was tired of renting and wanted to buy a building to house her real estate office, which was filled with antiques. She needed, she says, a very special environment that would "accommodate my business style." When she spotted the Gates house, she stopped her car at the curb, gazed long and hard and "I knew I had to have it."

"I didn't need to see it inside. I didn't know the history of the house. The broker had it listed as a Mizner," she says. Nothing mattered then except buying the place, which she did.

"A month after I bought it the roof in the kitchen caved in," she recalls. She repaired that and later added 1,000 square feet of interior space. "I put in central air conditioning," she says, "but kept the ceilings high." She also found new homes for many of the exotic trees and shrubs that practically hid the house.

It took until 1985 to find out the history of the little stucco house. By then Verna had restored the original polished oak flooring, chipped away the cork that covered the coral stone fireplace facade, and replaced six sets of jalousie windows with French doors.

She had discovered through searching old records that the house had been built around 1915 by Harley and Harriette Gates of Rutland, Vt., who honeymooned in Boca Raton and liked it well enough to settle.

Gates initially bought five acres of land near the ocean for $225. He later added another 26-acre tract and created Palmetto Park Plantation, a showplace for rare plants and fruit trees.

Gates encouraged friends and former Vermont neighbors to join him in settling the south and soon built up a healthy real estate business. He served at various times as a City Council member, a school trustee, municipal judge and historian.

Verna enjoys drawing comparisons between her real estate career and that of Gates. Harriette Gates also owned an antique shop, says Verna, who has placed photographs of the Gates atop the fireplace mantle, a place of honor in their old home.

Newspaper article on Morada Cafe

Second marriage with fainting groom

Fainting groom with paramedics

The Miami Herald

Purcell Search
May 20, 1978

'Vibes,' Vision Reopen

By TOM JEFFRY
Herald Staff Writer

Following the "vibes" of a friend and a psychic's vision, friends of missing pilot-doctor Anthony Purcell rented a helicopter Friday and began a search of islands in the Gulf of Mexico between Tampa and Cedar Key.

Although the official search for Purcell, the chief cardiologist at North Ridge Hospital in Broward County, and his twin-engine plane ended over two weeks ago, his friends took to the air after a Spanish-speaking Cuban psychic told them they would find Purcell there — weak and injured, but still alive.

But they returned to Tampa Friday night without having found Purcell.

LEADING THE search was Diane Dixon of North Miami Beach, a friend of Purcell, who describes herself as "sensitive of sorts." She said that she knew Purcell had to be alive, even though he has been missing on his flight from Pompano Beach to Panama City for almost three weeks.

"When I have strong vibes I've always known them to be true," Dixon said. Her vibes were so strong Monday that she called a friend who had a relative with supposed psychic powers to see if the relative could possibly help.

The next day Dixon went to the home of the psychic, whom she described as "a very religious woman." But the elderly, psychic was too tired to tell Dixon anything that night.

"She said one thing though — 'He's alive,'" Dixon said. On Wednesday night Dixon returned to the psychic's home hoping to find more about Purcell.

WITH THE psychic's daughter translating her mother's revelations from Spanish to English, Dixon said, she learned about Purcell's crash. "The only thing I told her was that a friend of mine had gone down in a plane," Dixon said.

With no more information, Dixon said, the psychic described Purcell, his plane and what he was wearing at the time of his crash. When the psychic began to describe Purcell's thoughts, Dixon said, she became convinced that the psychic was correct. "She didn't know his (Purcell's) personality before, and I did.

"The island that he's on is very small and when it's high tide it's almost covered," Dixon said the psychic told her. The right wing of Purcell's plane was protruding from the water, according to the psychic.

At the end of the evening, the psychic told Dixon it was urgent she find Purcell. She said the psychic told her Purcell was lying on the small island with a tourniquet on his leg and was weak from the loss of blood.

THURSDAY MORNING Dixon took the information the psychic had given her and went to some of Purcell's associates at the Lauderdale Medical Group. "She was so convincing when she came to us yesterday," said Virginia Ferayorni, wife of one of the doctors in the group.

"They felt they would never forgive themselves if they didn't go out and search again," Ferayorni said of the doctors in the office. That afternoon Ferayorni's son, Richard, and Dixon flew up to Tampa to renew the search for Purcell.

But after spending more than eight hours in a rented, $1,500-a-day helicopter combing hundreds of miles on the Florida Gulf coast, Richard Ferayorni and Dixon had not found Purcell. "We took our best shot at it and we didn't come up with anything," Purcell said.

Purcell took off from Pompano Beach April 27. Although he didn't file a flight plan, friends said they believe he was flying to Panama City. Radar contact with his plane was lost about 8 p.m. that night, when he was about 60 miles northwest of Clearwater. A search led by the Coast Guard was abandoned the next week.

A $10,000 reward was offered by members of the medical group to anyone who finds Purcell alive. They hope the reward will get local fishermen to go out and join the search.

FERAYORNI WAS debating Friday night whether he would continue his search today. "It's very possible we could have missed something," he said.

He said the helicopter flew just 200 feet above the water as they searched "island by island."

He said he believed the psychic after she described a rescue-flight pattern he flew two weeks ago while looking for Purcell. "Only my parents and the Coast Guard knew my flight plan," he said.

"It wasn't any kind of con," Ferayorni said. "She didn't want any money or anything."

Dixon said the psychic wished to remain anonymous. According to Dixon, the psychic uses her abilities to help only members of her family and close friends.

Both Dixon and Ferayorni were disappointed after the end of their search Friday. "We were so sure we would find him," Ferayorni said.

Major newspaper article on Dr. Anthony's disappearance

CHAPTER 7

Highway to Hell/Born Again/ First Adoption

I was now divorced, and I considered these past ten years a temporary distraction. When I look back now, I see it was God's safety net for those ten years. My soul's most dangerous journey would now begin. It would be a dangerous ride and, speeding on the Highway to Hell, I would be without God, His peace, nor with His safety net.

The pursuit of money and success continued with a frenzy. There were lots of my fair-weather friends who would meet me at the restaurant for dinner. Afterwards we would go clubbing. I knew my limits with alcohol and drove my own car. Just before the divorce was finalized, Thomas called to tell me he was diagnosed with a serious STD from his bar hopping activity.

I was tested and was okay. I informed the married man I was seeing and told him of the

STD alert. I continued using no discretion at all. I went from one affair to another. Some affairs lasted a year, some six months, or were one night stands despite the STD warnings.

I continued making more money, buying more properties, and overseeing my restaurant projects. I was asked to open an international real estate office in San Martin on the Dutch side of the Caribbean island of San Martin with a satellite office in Miami. When I was hired to do a review for a new project there, I celebrated my fortieth birthday. I was told about the money laundering happening on San Martin and on other Caribbean islands. I declined the offer and decided to continue with the foreign investors I was already working with in Florida.

One night I found myself alone in a bar I had not visited before with my friends. They told me about it. I went alone to check it out. I noticed there were hardly any women! One man asked me to dance and was very determined for me to be his trophy for the evening. As the bar was closing, he said, "Follow me over to my place." I heard a faint warning not to go! I paid no attention. Two days later I had a bad case of herpes. It stopped me in my tracks. I needed many weeks of treatment and lost all hope to recover. I considered that I could have been gang raped or murdered for that matter with all the unaccompanied "lions" in that bar. The pursuit of money, marriages, and affairs could not fill the large hole in my soul.

 A deep depression set in. I thought maybe I should just end it all. I thought about ways to do it. Through Our Father's merciful intervention, my journey came to a screeching halt. I had no choice but to stop and think about my journey. Our Father of love and mercy said enough! I wanted to remove myself from business and friends. The current project with just six lots out of 150 was soon going to end. The developer was pleased and liked by staff. I called the developer and told him I was going to take time off and that my staff who had been with me from the start would take over. He said no problem.

 I researched mountain retreats. I wanted the highest mountains that had quick access from Florida. I found one on the Carolina/Tennessee border called Roan Mountain. There was a state park with cabins at the top of the 6,500 foot mountain. I would be able to leave Florida with a change of planes in Georgia to a smaller aircraft that would land at the Tri-Cities Airport. I would then be able to rent a car at the airport and travel 25 minutes to the top of the mountain. I called and made reservations for three to four weekdays with the state park ranger and told him I wanted the largest cabin furthest at the top. I was told there was more activity on the weekends. I was not looking for activity. I successfully booked the largest furnished cabin in the park.

I was told by the park ranger it was fully furnished but that no food or restaurants were nearby. The park ranger said only six persons were allowed to occupy this, the largest of the cabins. He said I would have to walk a short distance from the parking lot. I thought that was perfect and booked the cabin and the flights. I landed at the Tri-Cities Airport late morning. I had reservations for the rental car and was quickly on my way to the one road leading to the top of Roan Mountain. I spotted a small grocery/produce store at the beginning of the road to the top of the mountain. I stopped and purchased food, produce, and bottled water to bring up to the cabin.

I arrived at the park ranger's check-in area for the cabins. There was a house near the parking lot for the park ranger and his wife. He checked me in and pointed out the way to the last cabin. He said, "This cabin only allows six persons. If more than five show up, I will have to turn them away." I responded that, as I stated when making the reservation, it was for one person, myself. The park ranger gave me the key with a very disbelieving look. During my first stay, the ranger and his wife were watching me every day to see if more people would arrive. That was okay, I felt safe knowing they were watching me. After I unpacked and fixed some breakfast, I decided to light the fireplace. I did not notice that the firewood was a little wet or that I might have to open a flue.

In just a little while there was a lot of smoke coming out of the fireplace. The cabin was full of smoke. I opened the door. The park ranger came running up and asked, "What are you doing?"

"I am so sorry," I said, coughing. I apologized and did not attempt it again.

The ranger noticed me walking the trails and warned me about the bears that were mating. I was also warned by his wife about the bees that she said were dangerous. I was allergic to bees and thanked her for telling me. She said these bees were on the ground with their hives and to watch where I was walking on the mountain trails. I never saw anyone up there because it was during the week. I brought snacks and would sit at the top of the mountain every day enjoying nature and the magnificent views.

In the evenings, I would sleep in the loft and would fall asleep listening to the night sounds of the forest from the small window near my bed. I did not get to ponder my journey. I was enjoying being alone with nature. The mountain was so beautiful and so quiet! I could not wait to book my next trip. I decided to book it when I went to say goodbye to the Park Ranger and his wife, and to return the key. My birthday was soon coming up so I booked for September 23 to celebrate my 46th birthday. I returned to work at the construction site and found all to be well.

Vera Marie Verna

I told the developer I was leaving again on September the 23rd. It was okay with him. My staff asked me where I went and who I went with. I said to a mountain by myself.

I knew they did not believe me! I felt more peaceful. No more nightmares, only dreams of that beautiful, quiet mountain. I was not up for work, the restaurant, or the office. Peacefully, I went from one task to another. I was wanting time to go by quickly so I could go back to the mountain.

When I arrived at Roan Mountain on September 23, I followed the same routine. I reserved the car and proceeded to the grocery store as I did before. I purchased some groceries.

The bill came to $11.00. I gave the girl at the cash register two $10.00 bills. She gave me back change but only $5.00. I told her, "Hello, I gave you two tens. This is not correct. You owe me four more dollars." She said, "No this is your correct change." I then insisted on speaking to the manager. He counted the register and apologized and gave me the $4.00. I think he had suspected her of skimming money. I had similar problems at my restaurant.

As I returned to the car, I was saying to myself, "Why did you make all this fuss for $4.00? Maybe she needed the money? No!" I said to myself, "That's not the truth. IT'S THE PRINCIPAL OF THE THING!"

As I drew closer to the state park, I increased my speed, trying to make better time. The road was empty of traffic. The car hit a tree on the side of the narrow road. I got out of the car to assess the damage. I thought, "Well this will cost a lot!"

I could even be overcharged with the estimate from the car rental office. Then I recalled that I did not take the insurance offered me in case of damage to the rental car! I thought I would just turn around, return to the rental office, and tell them I forgot to take the insurance. I had not been gone that long. I will sign for their insurance and avoid having to pay for the damage. I turned around and started driving back to the airport. As I was getting nearer to the airport, I heard a small voice asking, "What are you doing?" Not thinking about my answer or who was asking. I responded out loud, "I am going back to the airport to sign up for the insurance."

The quiet gentle voice said, "What about the incident just now with the girl at the register? You said it was THE PRINCIPAL OF THE THING! And wanted the manager to make good for $4.00? Did you forget that you said IT'S THE PRINCIPLE OF THE THING and for just $4.00?"

I turned the car around immediately and went back up to the mountain. That night in the loft it was so very quiet! I could hear noises of nature. I went back and reviewed where I had been for the last 46 years! I recalled each turn on my journey road. I recalled the womb experience with its nightmares. I remembered the good times taking care of my sweet little brothers and sisters, my good times at Notre Dame, and joining the Army.

I recalled the bad times, the two marriages, divorces, the fast driving on the Highway to Hell, and rejecting Him, Our Father, for those long 15 years. I was asking: *So Vera, what was the real truth about each turn you made on your journey?* Each time, I asked myself as Pontius Pilot did, "What is truth?" *What was the real truth, Vera?* It was a long revealing night in that loft! I realized that our merciful God had saved me from the airplane crash, STDs, gang rape, and violence. He saved me from a fatal accident on the Pan-American Highway with those dangerous hairpin mountainous turns without guard rails, not to mention violence and disease from my own rape.

I realized that even though I had abandoned God, He had not abandoned me! My search for money and success was completed but my soul had a big hole that I was not able to heal on my own. I recalled the words of Jesus, "I am the way, the truth, and the life." I thanked Our Merciful Father for putting up with me and asked Him to help me not to wander on that wide highway again! I promised God to ask for forgiveness for my sins and to help me not wander off the narrow road. If I did wander, and everyone wanders, I asked that I not wander for so long. I asked that I would be able to repent quickly from any sinful fall and not wait until the "Evil Referee" counted to ten over me!

Our Savior, Jesus, knew what it was to be tempted. I begged Him to keep me from any temptation to travel that deadly highway again. I believed He did forgive me and that I had to forgive all those that had trespassed against me. Jesus, who introduced the Lord's Prayer, was asking Our Father to forgive us our trespasses as we forgive those who trespass against us. When Peter asked Jesus if seven times was enough to forgive, Jesus said 70 times 7, and added that there would be a serious consequence if we did not forgive. That night I had a list going of those I had to forgive, all those who had hurt me after trying so hard to do the right thing for them. Even the rapist was on the list to forgive as I was forgiven.

That morning after checking out and driving to the airport, I planned to tell the car rental agent that I had damaged the car. What's the big deal, I asked myself? Just suck it up! IT'S ONLY MONEY! I would hear myself saying that again and again from now on. IT'S ONLY MONEY! I arrived at the airport and told the car rental agent that I seriously damaged the car.

He answered, "Do you have car insurance on your own car?" I answered yes. He said okay and fill out this form with your insurance information and we will take care of it. The ways of God are mysterious indeed. I was born again on my birthday. Now age 47, I understood that I had to test every single turn now on my journey. I trusted that Jesus, the Way, and the Truth would help me to do it.

I remembered the Bible where it was written about Mary Magdalene's plight. She was about to be stoned for her adulterous and sinful behavior according to Jewish Law, when Jesus asked her (after he told the stoners, "He who is without sin cast the first stone"), "Does anyone accuse you?" With all of her accusers gone, she answered, "No one, Lord." He said, "Neither do I accuse you. Go and sin no more!" I was encouraged by this Bible account, which is said to be the very words of God Himself.

Mary Magdalene did not only abstain from her sins, but became His follower, traveling with Him and the other women who ministered to His needs for three years. She, along with other women including His Mother Mary and John the apostle, were the only ones there when he hung on the cross for all those hours. I have come to believe that the Bible is the Word of God, and I read it every day to receive guidance. I learned that it has been the best seller every year! I was told that millions of dollars were reported each year from the sale of Bibles. I could see why and have read it every day now on my journey for guidance, especially before making any turns on the road.

Every day I ask that even my less serious sins be confessed and forgiven immediately to avoid any chance of being tempted to travel on that deadly Highway to Hell. I returned to Florida grateful and peaceful with my born again experience; I checked in at the Island Homes office to be sure I was not needed. I was in no rush to get back to my hectic routine as the project manager even though I only had six lots remaining. I was told that one of the couples was waiting for me to do their walk through before closing. They said they only wanted me to do their walk through and were waiting for my return. I instructed them to call the buyers to tell them I would set it up for this afternoon and confirm with the closing attorney that they would able to close afterwards.

I had the time confirmed for their walk through and closing. Only a few homes were still yet to close. Prior to the closing of each custom home, a walk through with each buyer was required to make sure all the custom finishes and any changes or corrections made were completed properly. Immediately after the walk through, the buyers' closing was performed on site with the developer's closing attorney. Copies of their signed documents were delivered along with their key so that immediate occupancy would be possible.

The couple showed for their appointment. I had spent hours with the architects and the two of them, finalizing their custom home. The husband had specific needs for a library and a home office. The wife also visited me at the office to do last minute changes to the pool area and chose a different type of tile she wanted throughout the house. She was lucky that I was able to make those last minute changes.

When they arrived with an infant, I asked "Whose cute little baby is that?" The wife said they had just decided to adopt and did not think an infant would be located so quickly! Neither did the adoption attorney. I replied, "Unfortunately we cannot change the library or the home office now." The husband said, "Don't worry. No problem. We will find a way to make do." They were so happy and I was happy for them, too. They were close to my age and had told me before they could not have children. They signed off on the walk through and closed. A few days later when I answered the phone, a woman identified herself as the adoption attorney for her clients who just closed on their home. They instructed her to call Vera Marie right away at this number. They told her I needed a baby, too! The attorney said she had an infant that would be born in a few months, if I was interested.

She said the sonogram could not identify if it was a boy or a girl due to the position of the baby. She said the cost would be $25,000. I told her I was 47 years old, single, and could not consider an infant at this time. She said to call her if I changed my mind before 5 p.m. tomorrow.

Infants were in demand 30 years ago, as so many in the area were lost to abortion. There was and still is a long list of couples wanting to adopt. Today, private adoptions are up to $50,000. There's no surprise that there is still a shortage to adopt infants either from private or public adoption agencies when you consider that 3,000 abortions occur every day in the United States alone. It is not surprising that some parents were going to other countries to adopt or added their name to the list of others wanting to adopt.

I decided to call a Catholic psychologist who was highly recommended. Fortunately she was able to see me with such short notice. My appointment was the following day at 11 a.m.

I explained I had to decide by 5 p.m. After I explained that I did not have children after 17 years of marriage and was now 47 and single, and I was offered a baby unsolicited, which I thought was unrealistic. I told her I needed assistance in order for me to give an answer to the adoption attorney by 5 p.m. She took a piece of paper and drew a line down the middle with titles at the top the top. "Yes" on one side, and "No" on the other side. We began with comments and discussions for each side at 12:30 and finished about 4 p.m. One comment was how will I take care of the baby as a single mother with no family around and long work days. She was young and had three children of her own. She said, "Have you heard about nannies and day care?"

Every issue and comment was noted on one side or the other. My age and relationship status was on the "No" side. By 4 p.m. the "Yes" column won. She asked me if I wanted her to call the attorney to say that Vera Marie had agreed to the adoption and for her to advise the next step. She made the call and I was to deliver the deposit the next morning.

The attorney said they still did not know the sex of the child, so I thought I'd name it Nicholas if it was a boy and Nicole if it was a girl. I did not have a problem getting to sleep that night. I was pleased with the psychologist who was a young, professional woman and practicing Catholic with children of her own. I was glad that she was able to give me an appointment on such short notice. She offered me answers to questions I asked her from my new perspective of being born again. I was satisfied with the outcome and gave thanks to Our Father for this blessing! No children after 17 years of marriage and now, at age 47, comes an unsolicited offer to adopt! Quite a surprise! Months later a baby girl was born.

Nicole had a life-threatening premature delivery. I was able to take her home after spending three days in the hospital. (The hospital gave me a room and wheeled her in so I could keep an eye on her 24/7.)

She was released to me on both an apnea monitor and a heart monitor with medications. I called several specialists and made appointments for their opinion about the heart medication and apnea issues. I called a cardiologist friend of Anthony's and he told me to take her off the heart medications. I did receive permission from the hospital to do so. I was assured that even though it was a traumatic birth, she would be okay. Several months later, I interviewed several nannies and found one. We practiced every day for a week with Nannie Jill at home.

I sure was that the nannie was okay, but I was not willing to take a chance leaving her at home since she was still on some medications. I called the developer and told him I needed to change one room of the model that was in the sales office. I told him I wanted to convert one room to a nursery. He said okay. I brought her portable crib and a sofa for the nannie to relax and read her magazines while Nicole was asleep. The office kitchen had a refrigerator for storing the formula, our food, and bottled water for guests and the receptionist. It was a perfect set up for us.

I was available for any questions from the nannie. I could check on her down the hall easily and often. I would pick up the nannie early and bring her to the model office with Nicole in her car seat. My morning routine had been to drive around the community on my golf cart for a quick, early morning inspection to check the stages for each custom home. There were over 140 custom homes completed and occupied, so not many to check on now. The builder would then stop by the sales office for coffee and report progress or answer any questions for each project. This was an extra service that I provided for the developer from the start. Now, there were fewer homes under construction and I was able to keep the routine with no problem. Some mornings when Nicole was not sleeping, I would put her in her car seat and drive her around with me.

She seemed to like the fresh air and the ride. The 140 owners were now set in their new homes. They were amazed at this novel scene. It became major news at Island Homes.

I completed the six homes in record time. The developer recommended me for other projects, but I declined. No more projects for me for at least six years. I purchased my dream home in a coveted area in East Boca Raton called Old Floresta. It had an all-glass office, which I converted into a music room, and I purchased a baby grand piano. It was a two story, five bedroom, four-bath home with French doors leading to the pool and gazebo area.

When Nicole was able to craw and speak, I set up swim lessons for her with an instructor. We met an elderly woman, Margaret, who had been a nurse and lived alone in a large home close by. Her community was a wealthy, guard-gated community. Someone from our church suggested that I call her as she was very lonely after her husband died.

She was not able to drive and was trying to take care of the large house herself. Her only son lived out of state and she did not want to bother him with her problems.

Nicole and I paid her a visit and she became Grandma Margaret to us almost immediately. She offered her assistance as a nurse when Nicole had pneumonia (seven times before her first birthday). We would drive her to shop for food and other errands. Margaret also played the piano but she did not have one in her large home. We shared the love of music. She would play my piano.

Nicole liked to listen to her play. Grandma Margaret would sit her on the piano bench and show her how to place her little fingers on the keys. I noted again how rewarding it was to have seniors and the young generations interact. It was good for Nicole and good for Grandma Margaret, and good for me!

Now, again I saw the value of seniors interacting with children. When Nicole would have her respiratory bouts, Grandma Margaret would sleep over at our house and sometimes we would sleep over at her house. She knew what to do and would often have me place her in the shower room and wait until it filled with steam and her breathing improved. Later with the breathing machine, she would help me with the treatments.

We celebrated Nicole's first birthday in my dream home. I invited a small gathering; one of my associates had an older child who doted on Nicole and brought her a fun game. Grandma

Margaret played Happy Birthday on the piano and we all sang along. It was a happy day for all of us. Shortly afterwards, she developed pneumonia again. That would make nine times in one year. Her doctors thought she had cystic fibrosis.

They recommended that I take her to St. Christopher's Hospital in Philadelphia. The doctor said St. Christopher's was working on a cure for cystic fibrosis and it would be the best place to take Nicole. They estimated it might take six months for testing or treatment. I wasted no time and put the house up for rent. I found a builder and his family who moved in right away.

They were waiting for their new home to be completed. They signed a lease for six months. I called to have the moving company pack up everything in a professional manner and told them I would want to leave it in their storage until I had secured my new address in Philadelphia.

My sisters and mother lived in South Jersey near the bridge that had access to Philadelphia, so I thought maybe I could find something in South Jersey. I scheduled an appointment with the hospital and would have Nicole's records forwarded to them by her Florida doctors. I closed the restaurant and put my realty business on hold.

The movers did a professional job packing our belongings. They took apart the piano carefully. The movers said they would deliver it all to our new location and unpack everything for us at our new destination. The owner of the company told me not to worry. When we were to ready to return, they would pack up and move us again. Nicole was on antibiotics but was doing okay for now. I booked the auto train from Florida to Virginia. I then planned to drive from Virginia to New Jersey.

We would stay with my sisters until we settled in our place in Philadelphia or South Jersey. I made sure the auto train cabin would have electric outlets to plug in her breathing machine if needed. We said our goodbyes and drove to the auto train.

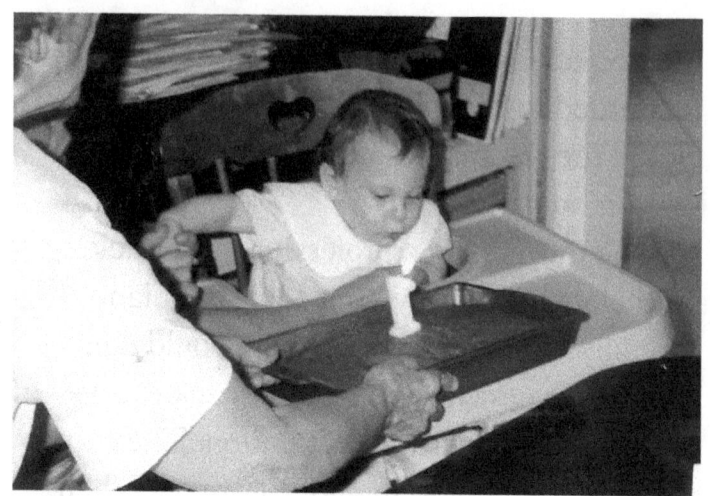

Nicole's first birthday at dream house

Nicole holding present on her first birthday

Vera and Grandma Margaret playing Happy Birthday in the music room

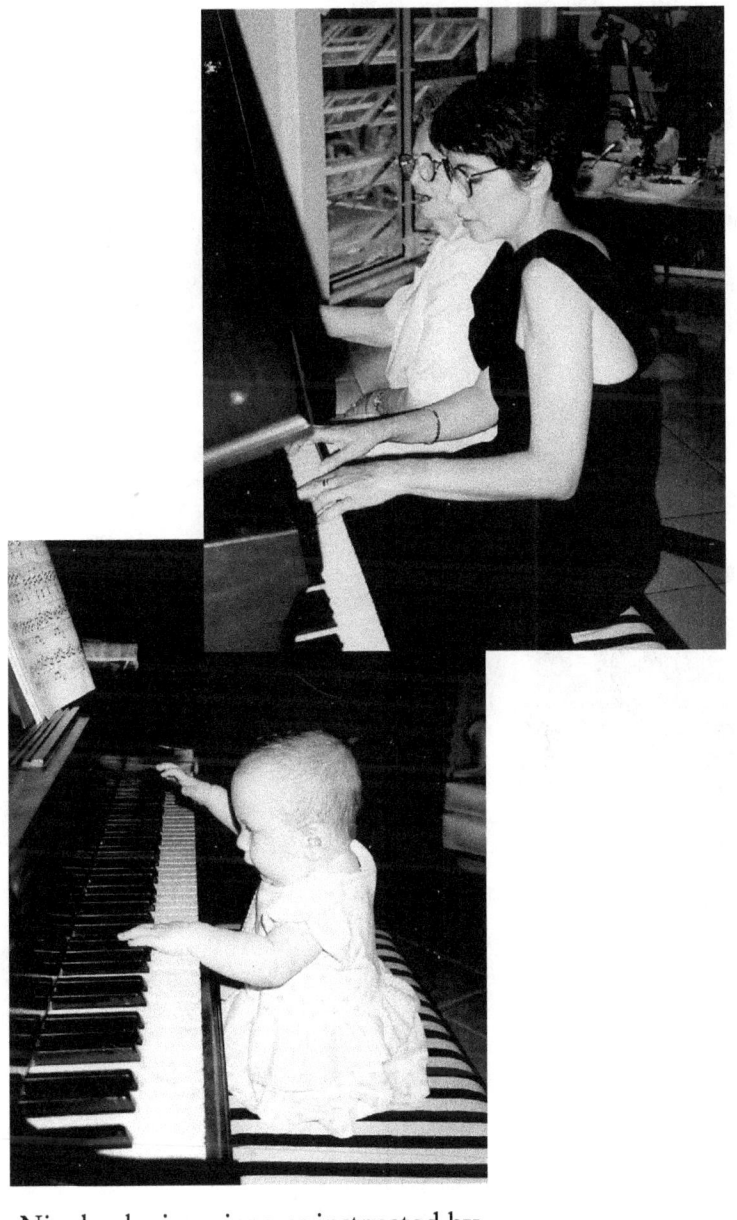

Nicole playing piano as instructed by Grandma Margaret

Two-story dream house

Client with adopted son, who told
attorney to call Vera Marie

CHAPTER 8

Hi Nella, Single Parents Ministry/ Mother and Child Art Gallery

When we arrived, I immediately started to drive around the surrounding area looking for a short-term rental. The rental companies were a "no go" on short-term rentals. I was very fortunate while driving around searching when I saw a house for rent sign on a little cottage in Hi Nella. I learned it was a very small town with some historical history. It was likened to a Norman Rockwell town in that no one ever sold or rented their homes. The town was a former Indian reservation. The address on the property was Pawnee Street. I learned that after the Pawnee Indians left or were forced to leave, others purchased the properties and liked the tiny town for its family-friendly atmosphere. Their homes were handed down from one generation to the next.

I called the number on the "for rent" sign and a young woman answered. She said her grandmother died at 100 years old and she had inherited the house. She said she was not ready to move yet and it had been vacant for some time. She decided to put the sign up for a short-term rental only. I told her that I would like to occupy immediately and would sign for six months. The granddaughter said okay. I told her we would take it. It looked so charming from the outside. The town was quaint and very small. I met her to sign the lease and was given the key.

The kitchen was on the primitive side with no provision for even a dishwasher, just a huge old porcelain sink and an old gas oven. It was so charming, with wood floors and a fireplace in the living room (which I never attempted to start up!). There were three bedrooms on the second floor and a basement equipped with laundry equipment. My antique furniture would fit in so well. I even had space in the dining room for the piano and china cabinet to hold my china, silver, and crystal glasses.

It did not have air conditioning but it did have a good heating system. There was a cute front porch and a nice backyard with a blooming cherry tree. I asked if I could repaint the living room, which was white and needed a little TLC. She said okay.

I called the moving company in Florida and since the boxes were already packed they said they would deliver in 24 hours. A hurricane in Florida caused some delay but the movers called again and said they would be there the following day. I decided to take Nicole's travel crib, her breathing apparatus, and the only clothes we traveled with. There was a sleeping bag for me that we had transported in our car. We would be ready for the movers who were to arrive the following morning. I called St. Christopher's Hospital to confirm again our appointment scheduled for the coming week. We went over to spend the night. Nicole and myself were sleeping upstairs. We were tired and fell asleep right away.

    I heard a very loud noise downstairs. I bolted down the stairs to the front door and saw neighbors talking on the sidewalk directly in front of our front porch. The cottage-like homes were close together. The antique street lights were on and I could see them clearly. I opened the front door and went out screaming, "Help! Help! There is someone in the house. Help! Call the police. My baby is in here."

The neighbors said, "Oh, we heard someone was moving in." It was only 9 p.m.! They said, "Stay here with us. We will call the police. We have never had a robbery in this town or trouble of any kind in Hi Nella."

They had only one policeman for the town. He was a heavyset, older man who arrived immediately. He quickly pulled out the largest handgun I had ever seen. It had to be an antique. He said, "Don't worry, Mom, I am goin' in to get her. Stay here." He then shouted to the neighbors to call for reinforcements from the neighboring town.

The neighbors tried to calm me down. They told me about the woman who lived in the house and that it had been vacant for some time. They said, "Welcome to Hi Nella! It will be okay, don't worry! We have never had a burglary or any trouble whatsoever in Hi Nella."

The second officer from the next town arrived and he too drew his gun (regular size) and went inside. Now I had completely lost it.

The neighbors kept telling me it was going to be okay; one woman put her arm around me. Then the heavyset policeman came out yelling, "I got her! I got her!"

He was holding up Nicole in his arms who was awake and looking around. The neighbors started to clap and cheer! They were saying oh how cute she is. Others were saying, she is just adorable!

The second, younger policeman came out. He said he knew the house had been vacant for a long time. He said that a raccoon had taken up residency in the basement. The officer said he closed the window and secured the door. He said he did not think the raccoon would come back after all the commotion.

The neighbors confirmed that a large, old raccoon was seen around the Hi Nella neighborhood. They were sure that was the case. They told me that it was a very safe place to live with hardly ever any disturbances. I had Nicole in my arms and was now trying to figure out how to carry her up the three steps to the porch and into the front door with my long night shirt. I explained I had to borrow it because our clothes weren't coming until tomorrow.

What drama! What nice neighbors! The next day, the neighbors asked the Hi Nella Fire Department to come and welcome us to their weekly pancake breakfast at the original old firehouse. We went the next Saturday and the firemen made a big deal welcoming us to breakfast. It was served on green, antique-glass dishes, which I was told were the original dishes.

They said that when they scheduled their next fire truck ride for the children around Hi Nella, they would contact me. The firemen issued a monthly flier and distributed it to the neighborhood with Hi Nella news. We were mentioned. The flier said, "Let's welcome Nicole and her mother, Vera, to Hi Nella." The neighbors brought cooked food and homemade cookies and cakes and welcomed us again and again, saying, "Now, don't you worry, we will look after you."

They did and when it snowed they would, without my asking, shovel the sidewalk in the front and the driveway. I had a little trouble with the heating and a neighbor arrived within

Vera Marie Verna

minutes. Wow, this really was like a Norman Rockwell town. Never, never would this have happened back home in Florida.

Our furniture arrived the next morning. The piano was set up and all my antique furniture, including the china, silver, and dishes, I arranged in my china cabinet. I decided to invite my family and some of my Hi Nella neighbors to the house for Sunday brunch. It would become a tradition every Sunday. I would cook most of it before Nicole and I left to go to Mass at the small, quaint church nearby. I had no dishwasher, but served them with my china dishes, silver, and crystal glasses. It was something I looked forward to every Sunday and the guest list changed as we continued.

After breakfast, they would insist on helping me wash and dry the dishes. Saint Christopher's continued with their testing. After four months, I was getting restless as I was used to always having so much going on. I decided to take the tests for real estate brokers wanting to hang their license in New Jersey and Pennsylvania.

I quickly passed the tests and then decided I did not want to leave Nicole to do business. I liked my life in Hi Nella, and having my family around, too. I did not admit it, but I was toying with the idea of staying here! I decided to put an ad in the local newspaper offering day care for children and seniors. I advertised that it would include evenings and Saturdays. The cost would be so much less than what was offered in Florida. A nurse, who would sometimes work evenings, was the first to call and showed up with a cute two year old. A waitress who worked some days, some nights, and on weekends brought her little boy and so it became a total of four children. There were no day care services that I know of in Hi Nella, much less those offering evenings and weekends.

I had one bedroom set up for girls and one for boys. I purchased some small beds in case they wanted to stay overnight or if they wanted to nap. I really enjoyed those four children and so did Nicole. A little four-year-old girl, whose name was also Nicole, came over to spend time with us. Her grandmother lived across the street and could not afford day care for her. This little one had a story.

When she was a toddler, she was burned with a hot cup of coffee. I had purchased a blow-up pool for the little ones to splash around in after their nap time. Little Nicole would not take her shirt off because of the horrible scarring on her neck and chest. She would not put on a bathing suit or even take off her shirt in front of anyone. She did show me later and it was pretty bad. I could understand why she would not take her shirt off or wear a bathing suit. She was very needy and benefited from being around Nicole and the other children. She enjoyed helping me with them. She was there with us now 24/7. Her grandmother started with allowing some sleepovers on only some nights, but then it was every night. She was so very sweet and wanted to be around me nonstop. I was never told why she was living with her grandmother.

One morning an elderly couple knocked on my door saying they saw the advertisement. They explained that they needed day care and were very lonely living at their apartment around the comer. They walked over. I don't know how they found me but the word was out in that small town. John and Mary were Irish and in their late eighties. They had seven children who all lived out of state with the exception of only one daughter who was somewhat of a distance from their apartment. She was a policewoman and did not have too much time for them. They had no car and said they would like day care or would even move in and pay rent. I told them I just did not have the room but I liked the idea. I told them they could certainly come over during the day and there would be no charge.

The next day they walked over and were so happy to be around the children. Nicole was their favorite. I brought my rocking chair and John would rock them for their nap and sing Irish songs to them. Mary had dementia and would just sit and watch all the action. She liked the stories that John would tell the children. John was always so careful with Mary. He would walk to get her fruit every day and helped her get dressed. They had been married for 50 years and he was so very doting.

I told him we would drive over when I wasn't busy with day care and would make breakfast for us. He liked potatoes with fried onions. He would read his Wall Street Journal while I was cooking for us. I would bring the food. He did not have a car and I started driving them to get groceries and whatever else they needed in that apartment. He tried to give me money, but I would not accept it. Nicole liked Mary. She liked to help her get dressed. Mary was very childlike with her dementia and Nicole realized it and made a special effort to help her. Nicole and I looked forward to breakfast with John and Mary. They needed special shoes for Mary that were only available at the mall. One afternoon I did not have day care, so I drove us to the mall. We brought Mary's wheelchair. Nicole would sit on her lap. I proceeded navigating around the mall. John was asking if they wanted ice cream. I wish I had taken pictures of this scene with Nicole on Mary's lap, both making a mess but trying to eat their ice cream together.

 When we were not busy at St. Christopher's and were free of other day care duties, we would drive over to sit awhile with John and Mary. John told me that he was worried that the family would put Mary in a nearby nursing home because of her dementia. Meanwhile they were invited to Sunday brunch along with our little friend Nicole and her grandmother.

Months later John's daughter said she was putting Mary in a nursing home. John said not unless he could go with her, too. There were a few beds for assisted living at the nursing home. The daughter was able to put them both there. We would go to visit and it was sad watching John trying to make sure Mary had fresh fruit and would cut up her food. He insisted on helping her dress.

Just before they both left for the nursing home, there was an Irish Festival at my little church. I invited them to go and they quickly accepted. They were the first to get up and performed the best Irish dancing I had ever seen. All eyes were on them. They received a great applause. I observed again what the elderly have to offer the young generation.

Now it was back to more regular hours with the four children in day care. The nurse and the waitress had worked their schedule around so that they were on regular afternoon and evening hours. My little helper, Nicole, was still helping me with the children. We were now able to have some structure with planning events in the afternoons. I found a horse farm down the street adjacent to Hi Nella.

After their nap we would take carrots and, with my little helper, we would walk the children to see the horses. Only one very old horse would hang out near the fence and each time we came to observe him, the little ones would bring a carrot. We could only observe the other horses from afar as they were on the other side of the farm. This was a highlight for everyone. We all looked forward to feeding the old horse by the fence. One day after feeding him a carrot through the fence, he collapsed! He rolled over on his back with his legs straight up in the air. The little ones screamed, "Poor horse! Maybe he wasn't allowed carrots! Maybe he's dead."

The horse, still on his back, started to move, his feet up in the air. He started scratching his back slowly, rolling over and over again with the little ones clapping as he did. I called the farmer as Nicole's second birthday was coming up and asked if he could bring the horse to her birthday party. He said he would but the horse was too old to ride. I told him that I would just tether him on a tree in the back of the house with food and water, and assured him that no one would attempt to ride him. He agreed and did not say how much an hour. I told him two hours. Nicole's birthday arrived. The parents of the children came to Nicole's party. I invited any of my family that chose to attend. I made a large sheet cake and we decorated the cake together. I created a fence with Popsicle sticks and the children placed some small animals I had purchased on the cake. I purchased five little cowboy hats for the children to wear with a red scarf bandanna for each to tie around their neck. The farmer delivered the horse with a little trailer. He said he gave the horse a bath, and would pick him up in two hours.

I tethered the horse in the backyard with the food and water the farmer provided. The tables were set up with the birthday cake and other foods I thought they would enjoy. These little ones said nothing about wanting to ride the horse but were fascinated, pointing to the huge feces that the horse was expelling in front of them!

They were being potty trained at the time, and were focused on this subject! I had no idea that the horse's feces would become the main event and highlight of the birthday party! The farmer came to retrieve the horse. I asked him how much do I owe, and he said no charge!

About a month before the party an older man called me about the advertisement I placed for senior and child day care. I did not run it again, so I surmised he must have held on to it. He lived alone in a house about ten minutes from Hi Nella. His wife was in a nursing home. He had a housekeeper but needed someone to cook and take him to the doctor. Nicole and I went over and told him we only had mornings and that I could cook for him and do his laundry. He liked the idea and we were hired, but only on days when we were not going to the hospital.

He was a poet and an artist. He was very happy to see us, especially Nicole. He and his wife had no children. If there was time, we would take him to his heart doctor or to see his wife in the nearby nursing home. He said, "Be a good girl and help your mother and I will buy you donuts." When I took him to his heart doctor, the doctor told me that Norman had only six months to live and he needed help taking his medicine on time. I told Norman that I would prepare breakfast, lunch, and dinner. He was scheduled to take his medications three times a day. I told him to do it with the food I prepared for the day, marked with "no microwaves," but he could put it in the oven. This worked out very well.

He was very happy and would start singing the song "How Great Thou Art." At Nicole's birthday party Norman drew a picture of the horse. I still have it. He also wrote a poem for me about an angel named Vera Marie, who was sent into his life by God. He was a good person and really missed his wife. Now it was six months and the hospital called to tell me Nicole did not have cystic fibrosis! She had another bout of pneumonia a month before. I was told then that the breathing treatments were just masking the true cause of her recurring pneumonia.

The hospital said the Florida doctors never gave her high enough doses of penicillin that were required to end the cycle of reinfection. The pneumonia would keep returning. They said it would now be required that she be admitted to the hospital to be monitored for high doses of penicillin. I stayed with her and she did okay with the treatment. I was grateful that this was discovered and thankful that they knew what they were doing. I called the movers who said to call to schedule our return.

    It was now time to say goodbye. I did not think I wanted to leave Hi Nella. I did not want to return to Florida and leave my new-found friends, my family, and my little church. I had to go back but told myself I would return to Hi Nella. How would I find a house there when no houses were for sale? I thought I would try anyway and planned to sell all the properties when I returned.

    I was happy with my new journey. When Nicole and the day care children would ask me to read to them, I had them learn nursery rhymes. One that was their favorite was Humpty Dumpty. The little children knew all the words to "my" version of Humpty Dumpty. They learned my version and recited, "Humpty Dumpty sat on the wall, Humpty Dumpty had a great fall. All the kings horses and all the kings men could not put Humpty Dumpty back together again, but God did!"

The Our Father became my favorite prayer. Having to be a responsible parent and hovering over my little one to be sure she was healthy and safe, I realized that Our Father in heaven is a parent himself and must have agonized over my senseless and dangerous wanderings on the Highway to Hell.

I had no desire to start a new building project. I decided to call the movers and would tell them to deliver my furniture to my empty two-bedroom house I owned and rented. It was now vacant. When I left, I did not have time to do the necessary painting and renovation to rent it again. I was so rushed to get to St. Christopher's. I realized now that even though I made up my mind to sell everything after paying off the mortgages, I would be forced to downsize. I thought it would be best to do it now!

I did not want to leave Nicole to return to my hectic work schedule until she was ready to start school. The same day, I was called by a neighbor who lived in the neighborhood. She told me people were picketing my dream house! Even coming by bus to picket the house at all hours of the day. I immediately called the tenant builder! He told me that he had a son who had been in jail for pedophilia and was now to be released. He said that was when the picketing started.

He did not know how the picketers came by the information. (I suspected it was the attorneys that lived there). The builder said he planned to leave the house in good shape and would not give me his forwarding address, in case I was asked where they had moved to. He was very distressed. He said his wife and family were traumatized and would vacate at night, as hundreds were picketing during the day! His younger son was tormented coming and going from the house as he was mistaken for the older son.

Apparently he made other arrangements for his son prior to his release. His son was not a minor so he would determine himself where he wanted to relocate. He said people were coming by bus loads. They were attaching fliers to the telephone poles with the son's picture and a summary of what he did.

Someone motivated the church adjacent to our neighborhood to protest as well. My associate phoned me to tell me it was written on a news report that the attorneys who lived there were looking for Vera Marie Verna, the owner of the house! The news stated that the attorneys were trying to get in touch with her to demand that she end the lease immediately.

This information would not have shown up on a security check as the son was not a minor and did not live with them when the crime occurred. I don't know which phone number they were calling! When I did get to speak to someone, they did not care that it was the wrong son and that it was just a six-month lease! I called the police to ask why they were not deterring the picketing. They said it was confirmed that the pedophile son was released but they had nothing helpful to add. Even when I arrived home in Florida, they were still picketing my empty dream house!

I was planning to sell everything anyway with my mind set on the office building. I had my broker's license secured to open in either Pennsylvania or New Jersey. I arrived back to Florida and my furniture was delivered to the two-bedroom cottage. I thought to sell most of the antiques before I left Hi Nella. They would not fit in the smaller house. I got good prices and even sold the piano! Why ship it back to Florida when I thought I would be returning to New Jersey? I kept only the essentials. The movers shipped it back within 48 hours.

We returned via the auto train and arrived before the movers did. After moving into the two bedroom, I put my dream house on the market along with the office building. The first person that called wanted it and arranged to meet me at the property.

After inspecting the house he was going to write me a check for the deposit when the misinformed picketers came by! The husband and wife took off! They were not interested even after I explained what happened. A single man who owned a successful business purchased it.

He said he traveled a lot—mostly out of the country. He would continue to live elsewhere. He was divorced and his children were older, married, and lived in the area. He said he liked the house and the price was right. He would wait to occupy it, and did much later.

When I received all the dramatic news in Hi Nella, I had decided to call the movers and advised them to deliver our belongings (now fewer) to my address at the two bedroom in Florida. This was okay as I intended to return to Hi Nella. I just did not know when. I lost money on the sale when I returned and sold it. I said to myself, IT'S JUST MONEY!

The two-bedroom cottage was very comfortable after doing some creative renovations. It did not have a pool but I had a professional build a playground with a tree house and a sandbox for Nicole and other children that lived close by. A little girl her age lived around the corner and would cut across the back to have access to Nicole and the playground. This was good as Nicole missed our family and all her little friends as much as I did. Prior to the closing on the sale of the building, my sister Bianca came to Florida with her little girl. I decided to have a barbecue at the building and invited a small group of friends.

The restaurant was closed but the equipment was still inside and it went well. I saw Bianca reading her Bible a lot and it was always with her. She suggested that I get one and to start with King David.

I did and then started over again at the beginning, reading it from cover to cover. I was not stressed at all with the move. I gave thanks that Nicole did not have cystic fibrosis. I was getting used to my role as mother. I think I was still in shock that after 17 years of marriage, I was able to adopt. It certainly changed my life. Little did I know what was yet to come!

I was just so relieved that Nicole did not have cystic fibrosis and thanked Our Father for the trip to Hi Nella. It was a life-changing experience. It was hard to say goodbye to family and the friends I met there. The worst was saying goodbye to my little helper Nicole. She said, "Please adopt me and take me with you!" I think I would have done so. Nicole would have a little sister, but living with her Grandmother was complicated. Who had the authority to allow me to do that or, for that matter, Who had power of attorney to even allow her to go with us for a visit? I thought I would come back anyway. The restaurant was closed and on my return I sold it. It sold quickly. I was thinking to return to Hi Nella but no houses were available for sale. What area of New Jersey could replace Hi Nella? I thought to stay in the two bedroom I already owned for now and then try to plan a return to Hi Nella. God had yet another plan that would soon be disclosed!

    I purchased a little rocking chair for my helper Nicole. I told her, "When you miss me, just rock in this little chair, it will help. I will try to come back." I gave her a hug and told her that regardless of her scarring that she was very beautiful inside and out and to remember that God would find another family for her to help as she did ours.

    I had to say goodbye to the little Catholic church, which I joined upon arrival. I was a member of their charismatic prayer group. There were only five members. The charismatic movement had just been introduced to the Catholic Church. Only one member of the group was a member of this church, beside myself. The other three were from nearby churches in the area that did not have charismatic prayer groups. I learned a lot about charismatic worship. They met once a week on Tuesday. There was no room to accommodate the small group meeting. The pastor allowed five chairs to be placed on the altar for us to meet.

I never missed their weekly meetings. I was impressed with their robust praise and meditation on the Scriptures. After the meditation and prayer for everyone's petitions, they would witness to how the Lord had worked in their lives that week. When it came to my turn to witness, I would just decline, saying nothing! I was, after five months, still taking it all in. The charismatic experience was still new to me. Notre Dame never showed us how to pray that way and to meditate on Scripture. I thought it was a wonderful and exciting approach to worship.

When I returned to Florida, I joined a charismatic Catholic church a short drive from my home. (I went to Mass there with Nicole and the other two that were to come to be raised at that church.) When I said goodbye to the Hi Nella prayer group director, she gave me her phone number to keep her posted. I called to tell her I had joined a charismatic church and a charismatic prayer group. I told her it was wonderful and that I was now able to share after the meditations. She said, "Wow, you are talking at last!" I never said one word of comment in those meetings for the group. My friends in Florida now would be startled that I was never able to comment or speak a word when asked to do so beforehand. They could never imagine Vera Marie at a loss for words and speechless! I was still reading the Bible every day and found it to be an experience, meditating on His Word, which He was not reluctant to share with me in my times of distress.

After my born-again experience, I was getting the whole picture but still very slowly. With Nicole's adoption, I was forced to move on to other pursuits besides money. I was glad about the rescue from the Highway to Hell, but still did not fully understand. After being out of work for six months, I closed the restaurant and put my real estate business as project manager for new projects on hold. The Hi Nella experience was necessary to discern and grasp what was important back then and now what was not. My priorities changed. Hi Nella helped me. I found myself more appreciative and respectful of all life. The babies, the young, the old, and for sinners like me still fighting my own addictions to sin.

    I had a small glimpse of God's plan for His Creation and for me. The successful interaction with various seniors and children in need prompted me to join the single parents ministry at a Catholic church nearby. This proved to be a very rewarding experience. There were only 11 members of the group and each had one child like myself. Some of them were fathers and mothers whose spouse had died and now were single parents. The others were mostly mothers divorced with a child. I was the oldest single mother. The group attended Mass every Sunday and we would all sit together with our children. My daughter so loved these Sundays when she could play and celebrate birthdays with other children. I had the tree fort and playground set up already.

    I thought to invite the single parents: Nannie Jill, Grandma Margaret, and my next-door neighbor who was widowed, to attend a brunch with the singles and their children after Mass. All of them showed up after Mass with their children. No exceptions. The singles group would participate together in other activities on Saturdays together. We would go as a group to the local parks for a barbecue or to water parks, the movies, or the zoo. All the holidays were celebrated together for that year. They could leave the luncheon at any time but did not choose to do so.

It was a church ministry for single parents only. The members had trauma from one thing or another. From a young spouse having died or from having sole custody now for their little ones. They were trying to adjust. I found their main concern was for their children. They immediately accepted my offer to have brunch and playground time for their children. I would prepare quiches the night before and would heat them up when we got back from church just around the corner.

I made hard-boiled eggs, purchased donuts for the children, and of course had lots of small cartons of milk and orange juice. They were always in a hurry to go out back to the playground. We were able to monitor them with the sliding glass door at the rear.

I turned the large coffee maker on before I left for church so that it would be ready when they arrived. No china and silver now (all were sold). I used paper plates, cups, and throw-away spoons and forks. The children would grab some food and immediately wanted to go play at the massive playground and tree house. They would pop in and out for a quick drink. In the meantime, the single parents would talk with one another about raising children. The single moms, dads, and the seniors would always have an immediate concern or two to discuss for the past week or for the upcoming week. The single moms and dads would exchange information about referrals to day care, pediatricians, and medications for themselves or their children.

    I noticed that all the questions and concerns of these singles were discussed in depth with patience and sincere concern. The widowed women were enjoying giving advice to the moms and dads about every issue and were glad to answer their questions in detail. These needy singles were very interested in what they had to say! Most of their own parents were not local or available.

    No one was ever in a hurry to leave! The brunch always lasted for one to two hours! This went on for over six months with the same participants.

It was now summer vacation. I thought it would be good for myself and Nicole to take a few weeks and drive up to New Jersey to visit my mother. She had not seen Nicole in a while. I thought I would invite mom to a bed and breakfast to celebrate her upcoming birthday. We started the drive up there and looked for little rural towns on the way and asked thereafter if there was a bed and breakfast nearby. Surprisingly, the bed and breakfasts were located in the rural areas and we found them to be very clean and inexpensive. We would walk around Main Street in each town, sampling the local food. I wanted to collect Mother and Child art. I thought to create a Mother and Child gallery and use it for fundraisers for my first nonprofit: the Foundation to Support Mother and Child, Inc. I had incorporated the nonprofit and thought it would be a good idea to look for art and other items, jewelry, statues, etc., for the gallery. I was surprised to find many pieces of art.

The church with the single parents ministry was going to have an auction and sale. I thought I would contribute articles of Mother and Child to be sold and the proceeds given to the single parents ministry on Sundays. One Sunday we found a little Catholic church in North Georgia near the rural bed and breakfast. The scenery was beautiful. The church was old and very small but full of friendly parishioners that greeted us with enthusiasm! I was thinking maybe they did not have too many visitors. It reminded me of our Hi Nella experience.

After the service, the priest gave us a blessing and welcomed Nicole and I to follow him over to a park where they would have their picnics after Mass! The parishioners would cook and bring their homemade local delicacies each week! Every age group had something to do. There were potato-sack races, swings, and sliding boards at the park. The men set up the tables. The women brought tablecloths and picnic gear and served the delicious food to everyone. We stayed all afternoon and when we were leaving it seemed like they had adopted us! They asked us to move there. They said they would love to have us join their community! Wow, another Hi Nella experience.

We continued with bed and breakfasts, finding them easily in the rural areas. On their main streets I found more art and items for the auction. At one stop off the main road, we found a bed and breakfast with an adjoining Caraval-like sliding board, but with water provided on the slide to keep it cool and comfortable. We stayed several days. Nicole had met a little girl her age to hang out with. The little girl was the only daughter of the owners. She played with her little friend's dog for hours and they would wade in the creek nearby on the grounds of the bed and breakfast, spending hours going down the water slide. The owners assured me she was very safe with their daughter and were pleased that she found a friend. I myself enjoyed walking down the road to pet the cows and their baby calves there at a farm. She said goodbye to her little friend. They gave each other a hug goodbye. Nicole told me she wanted a dog, too!

We arrived in New Jersey and told mom all about it. I looked for a bed and breakfast and found one near the famous Cow Town Rodeo. We arrived in time for the rodeo. Everyone in the town was wearing cowboy hats! The town was rural and the bed and breakfast was a little pricey, but it had excellent amenities. I saw a sign when we checked into the bed and breakfast. It said, "Horses available to ride at their own barn." Nicole had been riding horses and ponies since she was two years old. When I hired instructors to teach her to ride, they would always say she was a natural in the saddle. After breakfast, I told mom that I wanted to see about a horse for Nicole to ride, and then we would checkout and take a tour of main street. Mom said okay as she was finishing her coffee and watching Nicole who was content playing with the kittens belonging to the owners of the bed and breakfast.

I found the barn but there was no one there! I walked into the barn and to my surprise on the far wall was a large, beautifully framed picture of a Mother and Child! I had never seen this image before and it was unsigned. The artist had painted it with both the Mother and the Child gazing forward with a captivating gentle stare. I was determined to purchase it. What was it doing in a barn anyway? It was leaning against the wall on a large workbench.

Upon entering the barn you could not miss their gaze even if you wanted to.

    I was told at the front desk that the bed and breakfast owner was in, and they told him I would like to speak to him. I asked if the framed picture in the barn was for sale. He said he purchased it for the frame only and was working on it in the barn. I asked if I could purchase the picture. He said, "$150 and keep the frame." I gave him the money and walked back to the breakfast room to show mom the picture. She said, "How much did you pay for that picture?" I told her and she asked, "Why so much? What is so special about it anyway? It's not even signed by the artist." I told her the gaze of the Mother and Child sold me. Afterwards, we drove back to her house where we were to spend the night. I placed the large, framed picture on her foyer table against the wall. When we woke up the next morning, mom was already up and said, "My goodness that gaze is really something. I cannot walk by without reacting." We left for Florida. I had purchased quite a lot of items for the auction.

    I decided to have sepias made for this very old picture at a nearby photo lab. When they removed the frame to make the sepias (in browns and black), it could be reprinted and framed for sale. I was told that it was so very old that it was hard to remove it from the frame without destroying the picture! They did so carefully with just one small pin-size mark showing! The auction and sale was a success and every item was sold. The proceeds were donated to the single parents ministry. I kept the sepia copies and offered them in whatever tones the buyers desired, browns or black tones.

    I had several wine and cheese parties at my home art gallery and would take orders. I sold every single original one! I had them put the original picture back in the frame. I found out later that the image was well-known. I never asked how much it was worth. I used the picture for the logo for the Mother and Child art gallery. I still have it to this day and it is one of my treasured possessions. The St. Michael Art Gallery in Georgia had been in contact with me when I ordered several copies of their Mother and Child art. They told me they were going out of business and had a large canvas copy of Our Lady of Guadalupe signed by the bishop of Guadalupe and asked if I would be interested in purchasing it at a closeout price. I did, along with other copies of Mother and Child art they were selling at closeout prices. The Our Lady of Guadeloupe was very special for me. It depicted Mary with Mexican features, pregnant with Jesus, and wearing a certain tie or ribbon on her dress used by the Mexican women at that time to identify that they were pregnant.

    The Mexicans of Guadalupe celebrate her on December 12 every year with mariachi bands in front of the church that was built where she appeared to a poor peasant, Juan Diego. It is a very well-known image and she was instrumental in saving the Mexican babies who were being offered for sacrifice to pagan gods. I still have the original I purchased from them. I had copies made, some smaller than the original one, and framed. They sold out immediately, each time at every art presentation at whatever location we were presenting Mother and Child art.

    I received a call from my little brother Patrick. He told me years ago that he had AIDS before moving to California. He called to tell me he was now terminal and asked if he could come down to be with me. He still owned his condominium that I had purchased and rented annually. It was available.

Patrick was happy when I adopted Nicole, but he was not able to meet his new niece. I told him it would not be a good idea to expose her. At the time, much was not known about AIDS. I told him that I would travel to California to be with him. I called places in Florida that rescued men with AIDS. One Catholic home nearby that rescued men told me when I called that they had a full house, but that I should not be afraid to have him fly down to stay near me at his condo. I thought he probably knew more about the disease than I did. I called Patrick and told him to come down right away.

I was expecting him to arrive in Fort Lauderdale when instead I received a call from him saying that his lungs were so bad that he had to be hospitalized when the airplane stopped over in Georgia. He said he was still in the hospital. He asked if I still wanted him to come to Florida. I said, "Of course you have to come to be with me." It was confirmed that he was dying.

His medicine was available here for him but would not do much to relieve his condition. He finally was discharged. He arrived and gave me a big hug. I was able to be with him for those few months before he died. I would take him to the AIDS clinic nearby for his medications.

On one appointment I had my little one with me. When I turned my head to observe what he and a nurse were saying, she decided she would put her little hand in the bright-red toxic wastebasket to investigate what was in this colorful box. I screamed and soon several nurses came running into the room. They checked her and double checked her thoroughly for puncture wounds. This was the toxic wastebasket used to dispose of the needles given to the AIDS patients! Patrick and I were both shaken even when they said no puncture wounds were found on her little hands. Patrick was so upset and almost in tears. He was not recovering well from this incident even though the nurses said that she was free of any punctures. He insisted that if I came to visit, to come alone as he did not want to put his little niece at any further risk. He stayed by himself for a while.

When Patrick arrived, he was all the "New Age" religion, meditating and such. I was determined that he'd be born again as I had been. One Sunday, I asked the church to set up an anointing for him as he was dying. I told them that I had called several times and left messages but was not successful. I was told that all week they were being visited by the bishop and his staff and were sorry that they could not respond. An assistant to the deacon said, "Give her some anointing oil to use to pray over him, and schedule him for the next priest available to complete the anointing." A small cloth dipped in the oil was presented to me.

I quickly drove to Patrick's condo and told him what I was told about the anointing and the priest that would visit him. I told him that his Father in heaven wanted him to have it.

I asked for his permission to pray and anoint him with the little pad soaked in the oil and he consented. We said the Our Father, which he remembered as he was fully catechized in our family church and knew all the prayers. I brought him a Bible and he always had it in his hand when I went to visit. He was sometimes reading it when I would arrive. I asked him what he was reading and he always said the Gospel of John. He thanked me for bringing the pad of anointing oil and said he was looking forward to the priest.

Within the next few weeks, it was necessary to have an ambulance bring him to a hospital about 20 minutes from his condo. After a few days, the priest came to the hospital after I set up the time. I was not present, but Patrick told me it was long overdue and he wished he had requested it years ago. He seemed very peaceful. I received a call from the hospital a little later in the week and was told he was dying, that I should come quickly, and he was waiting for me. He did not want any morphine for the pain. He told the nurse he wanted to be lucid when I came to say goodbye. Back then, with not much information about AIDS and contagion, none of my friends wanted to be around me and Nicole. They did not want to babysit or even engage in close-up conversations with me. I still did not know much either about the contagion issue so I was not upset about it.

One friend who worked for me for several years knew Nicole since I adopted her and reluctantly agreed to babysit. I explained I needed to go to the hospital right away and that my brother was dying. She checked with her husband and said to drop her off but to be back by 9 p.m. I was grateful. It was 5 p.m. when I left to travel the turnpike, and it should only have taken 15 minutes to arrive at the hospital. I called to tell the nurse that I was on my way and to let my brother know. I encountered a bad accident on the turnpike and all traffic was backed up. I got there at 6 p.m. and told him what happened. I told him my associate would take care of Nicole until 9 and that I was grateful that I could drop her off at their home.

    We talked for some time about his growing up and all the things we liked to do together. He thanked me for taking care of him and for sending the priest over to the hospital. He said he worried about my single parent adoption of Nicole. His legs were going numb. He asked me to massage them, he thanked me, and said it helped.

    His breathing was very bad and the pain was increasing. He called for a morphine shot. The nurse informed me again when I arrived that he was refusing morphine shots while waiting for me to arrive. He received the shot and proceeded to die, saying he wanted me to pick up his little niece.

As he passed we recited the Lord's Prayer. I said my goodbyes to my lifeless little brother, closed his eyes, and called the nurse. She told me that Patrick was so polite and a perfect gentlemen. He thanked her and the doctors for their excellent care. She said he was waiting for me and told her I was more of a mother than a sister to him. I said my goodbyes again to my lifeless little brother and whispered in his ear that I would see him in heaven.

I was back by 9 p.m. to pick up my little one. I called the next morning to advise my mother and relatives of the date for the funeral and internment. I found and paid for the crypt. I was overjoyed that I was able to be with him and to help him back to his heavenly Father before he passed. I would miss him so much. He had given me power of attorney to sell his condo and to take care of his expenses. I was asked to pick up his ashes so the funeral would not be delayed. When the ashes were ready, I was asked if I needed help carrying the ashes to the car. They said it was heavy. (He was over six feet.) I replied, "No thank you. I will do it." He's not heavy, he's my brother! I placed the ashes in the front seat and put the seat belt around them, singing him deliverance songs all the way back to the funeral director, who was pleased that the service would not be delayed and drove them over himself.

When Nicole celebrated her fourth birthday, I was serious about adopting a little sister for her. We had no family here. I thought it would be beneficial to share her childhood with a little sister to grow up with and to experience a family. I called a woman from our prayer group in Hi Nella who worked for an adoption agency. She said the least expensive private adoptions were running about $17,000. It was much less than Florida, but I told her I could not afford even that. She suggested that I call Mother Teresa's orphanage in India.

I purchased the original Mother Teresa movie and it featured Mother Teresa with her orphanage. I don't remember how I found her number in India. I made sure to call on India's time at 8 a.m. When the operator answered, I asked to speak with Mother Teresa. I noticed the operator was using the old plug-in system.

She was plugging in to several numbers to try to find her! Finally the operator said, "Oh, she must be at her convent as she was not feeling well," and plugged me into the convent. The first nun that answered could not speak English. When I asked for Mother Teresa, she found another nun who spoke very good English. I asked to speak to Mother. She conferred that Mother was not feeling well but asked if she could help me. I proceeded to tell her that I was a single mother, getting up in years, and wanted to adopt a three-year-old girl to be a little sister for my adopted, four-year-old daughter. I wanted my daughter to have some family she could grow up with. I asked if that was possible. The nun said, "Yes, of course. We have a lot of three-year-old girls." She said, "As you know the girls in India are aborted and most people want to adopt boys. How many three-year-old girls do you want?" I replied, "Just one for right now." I asked how much it would cost and told her I only had $7,000.

She said Mother Teresa does not charge for adoptions. She said the process for the family wanting to adopt was to send a picture of their family and to identify the gender, age, and how many they wanted to adopt. Some request a certain gender and age and some request more than one child. This also helps to confirm availability before they travel to India. For the ones that cannot travel to India, Mother Teresa or her nuns bring the matched child to New York. She said Mother has a convent there in New York and routinely brings children there. She asked if I wanted to send a picture of my family so she could try to match a selected three-year-old girl for Mother Teresa to bring to New York. I told her my family consisted of myself—a single mom with dark brown hair and brown eyes. My adopted daughter had big blue eyes and blonde hair. I told her I knew that the children in India had brown eyes and to just pick the one for me that had the biggest brown eyes! She laughed and said, "Okay, I will do it!"

    I gave her my address and phone number and she said she would be contacting me soon to advise me about Mother Teresa's next trip to New York. Nicole was excited. She had me buy a little bed to put right next to hers in the second bedroom. She decorated it with a new bedspread and said she would share her large dresser with her new sister. She was so looking forward to a little sister! She had watched the original Mother Teresa movie with me, which showed Mother's orphanage. She watched it several more times now to see what those in the orphanage looked like and said: "Maybe one of these kids will be the one Mother Teresa brings for us!"

Mother & Child Art Gallery

Mother and Child framed picture found in the B&B barn

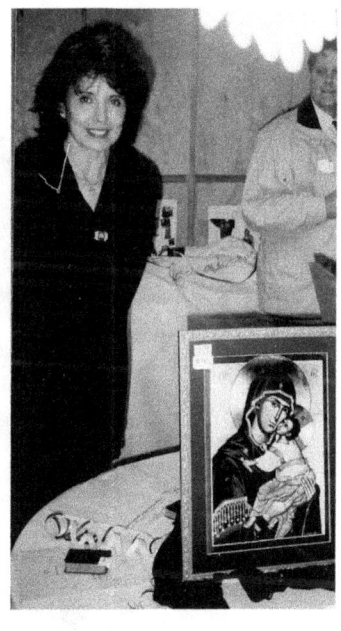

Photos of Hi Nella house

Nicole's second birthday with
farmer delivering the horse

Nicole's second birthday
with helper Nicole and the horse

Nicole's second birthday
with rodeo cake

CHAPTER 9

Second Adoption/Mother Teresa/ Sister Philip Marie Burle

Nicole and I were waiting for news from Mother Teresa's convent in India as to when we would be able to pick up the three-year-old girl that was being brought to New York. I was introduced at this time to Sister Philip Marie Burle who was giving retreats at a church in my area. She gave retreats to Mother Teresa's nuns in India and had met Mother Teresa there. She encouraged me and showed me pictures of her retreats in India. She traveled all over the United States and Germany, giving retreats nonstop. I offered to help her with them and, for 21 years plus, assisted with cooking "Angel Eggs" for all her retreats in north and central Florida. Advertised in all the bulletins: Serving "Angel Eggs." Not deviled eggs. Everyone wanted to know about them. It was made with no cholesterol, stuffed with hummus, and were a hit with the community. It was my delight to be able to serve with Sister Philip Marie!

I received a message from a former client who purchased an ocean property. He left a message that his next door neighbor wanted to sell a property by the ocean, which was owned by his mother. He said he recommended my agency to sell it. An appointment was set up. I met the man at his home office in his ocean mansion.

He had his own private jet and was flying back and forth to France for his new tech company, which was supplying training for new emerging technology. He also funded music events and popular artists at the convention center. These were just a few of his other businesses. He was very well-known around town, for his diversified business skills.

He began the meeting by telling me that he had two young sons with his second wife and she was complaining that her sons and his nephew were competing for his time. She complained that he spent little time with his family, because he was often away on business and this was not acceptable. She said she no longer wanted to share the care for his nephew, who was now ten years old. He said the boy's mother died nine years ago in a tragic hit-and-run accident and the father could not be found. He was sharing the care for his nephew along with the boy's grandmother, who was elderly. He said that he wanted to sell her ocean condominium just down from his home. He had been trying to find a boarding school for his nephew but had not been successful. When his neighbor next door told him I was adopting from Mother Teresa's orphanage, he decided to ask me to put his condominium on the market and asked if I wanted to adopt his nephew! He said his neighbor had all good things to say about me and thought I would make a good mother for his nephew. He said, with a grin, that he wished I could be his mother, too. I told him I was a single mom with a two-bedroom home and was expecting to receive a call soon for a three-year-old girl from Mother Teresa's orphanage. I explained that I could not accommodate his nephew in the two-bedroom home, and since I was a single mom, I thought it best to stick with just girls. I explained I wanted a sister for my adopted daughter and a little sister would be a way for her to grow up with family when I was gone.

I suggested that he sell his mother's ocean condominium but not to place her in assisted living. With the proceeds from the sale, he could purchase a small villa close by for his mother and nephew to live in. The cost of assisted living was high and boarding school would be expensive as well, if he found one. Instead of paying the very high costs of assisted living and boarding school for his nephew, he could hire a cook and live-in housekeeper as needed.

I told him I experienced dramatic results and benefits when seniors and children interacted with each other on a daily basis. He responded, "Absolutely not!" He said he would put his mother in an assisted-living facility and would have to find another place for his nephew until he was old enough for boarding school.

He then told me he was investing in a movie featuring the life of Mother Teresa. He said it would be best to wait until after she died to fund the movie. He told me that the adoption laws had changed for India and that Mother

Teresa could no longer bring babies directly to New York or any country for that matter. He said it was now required to go through an adoption agency and to travel to India. "Why not just take my nephew?" At this point, I thought I should not be doing business with this man. I picked up the listing contract and put it back into my brief case. I did not believe for a minute what he said about Mother Teresa and the adoption laws in India.

He saw that I was getting ready to leave. I watched as he swirled his chair around to his filling cabinet behind his desk. He took out the short preview to the Mother Teresa movie. It had a picture of Mother Theresa on the movie case. He said, "Here take it!" When he put the movie in my hand, I heard a voice say, "Take this one, Vera." It was so loud in my mind that it stunned me. For a few moments, I just stood there staring at her picture. I was convinced he was wrong about the change in India's adoption laws for sure, but I found myself saying, "Okay, I will adopt your nephew."

He looked shocked, but replied quickly, "Pick him up today at 5 p.m. I am leaving for France tomorrow. I will tell my secretary to give you whatever you need and to tell her to start the adoption immediately." I left thinking he was wrong about the adoption laws changing and that I would be able to get Nicole her little sister. I thought I would just have to find room for Brandon. At 5 p.m. I picked Brandon up at his grandmother's, and met him for the first time. He was very cute and friendly. He did not look like ten years old at all. He was so very thin. His bones were showing through his shirt. (Later I found out he was bulimic and suicidal from his elementary school teacher who said she reported it, but nothing was done about it after meeting with his family.) She said she was so concerned that she would have adopted him herself if her husband would have permitted it. On the way to my house, Brandon was so talkative. He said, "Oh look at that beautiful sunset. Do you like sunsets? I would take a picture of that if I had a camera. Do you like photography? So I am going to live with you, great! But why are you driving this old station wagon? My uncle has more than one car and his favorite is the Lamborghini."

Brandon told me about his uncle's boat and airplane. He said he was not invited much to family gatherings or family boat trips. He said he had been living with all of his out-of-state relatives for short periods of time, except for his uncle's brother who was very violent and always angry.

He liked staying with his grandma. He liked going across the street to the ocean with his surfboard and to his cousin's house down the street. They liked to surf there as well. He asked, "What's for dinner?" I told him turkey with mashed potatoes, gravy, and homemade apple pie. He said, "Wow, my favorite!" I picked up Nicole from day care and she was surprised to hear he would now be part of the family.

I showed him the house and told him about the three-year-old girl from Mother Teresa's orphanage in India that we were expecting to adopt and who was to arrive very soon. She would be staying in Nicole's room. He said, "Oh, I see you have this very large, enclosed porch with a window air conditioner. I could make that my room and would like to paint it. It is larger than the one I have now."

He ate everything and asked for seconds. (He was always asking me thereafter to make this same meal every week, especially the homemade apple pie). He asked that I make him his own in addition to the family pie. I told him I had to get him back to his grandmother's house to pick up his clothes. He asked, "Could I bring some leftovers for Grandma?"

We arrived at his grandma's house and she put it in her empty refrigerator! She was so very thin herself! There was absolutely nothing whatsoever in the refrigerator. She said, "Yes, I will pack up tomorrow. I am going soon to assisted living so I have to go through everything for myself, too. I will have his things ready tomorrow. He will sleep here and you can pick him and his things up tomorrow."

The next day I dropped Nicole at day care. It was a Christian day care and she enjoyed going there, but it was just on certain days and her pick-up times were flexible. When I stopped to pick up his things the next morning, (I had to make several trips as his bike and surfboard just barely fit in the station wagon), the condominium manger stopped me. He said, "Oh, you must be the lady who is going to adopt Brandon." He thanked me for taking the boy. He was very concerned himself about him. He said Brandon was always wandering around at all hours of the night on his bike. He said his grandmother has thrown out a lot of boxes of trash, and one box with no cover was blowing medical papers around. He thought I might need some of those papers. He salvaged those medical documents about Brandon's traumatic birth and his many surgeries.

I was so happy and forever grateful to him for salvaging them for me. I noted that Brandon was in and out of the hospital for the first two years of his life. I was glad to have this paperwork, especially the documents on his heart surgery. The hospital notes stated that he was born with a narrowed aorta heart valve, which required immediate surgery. I was soon to notice this when he took off his tee shirt. I saw the scars across his back and I was reminded of my little helper Nicole who would not take off her tee shirt because of her extensive scarring. The paperwork helped when I took him to a heart specialist to check it out. He had not been to a heart doctor since! God had a plan when he presented Brandon to me for adoption.

Within a year of being monitored regularly by a cardiologist, I was told he needed emergency surgery again. The cardiologist who did his surgery said he could have dropped dead at any time! It was thought when he was an infant that one surgery would be enough to make the correction, but the procedures they used to make the corrections were now outdated and no longer used. His cardiologist sent a referral to Miami Children's Hospital with the records to present him for emergency surgery.

When we arrived at the hospital for the procedure, the surgeon, after he had been under anesthesia for one hour, came out of the operating room to tell me they could not stabilize his heart and thought they would have to put in a pacemaker first. I prayed and tried to stay calm. After another half hour, the surgeon came to report that he was stabilized without the pacemaker, but required a stent implant to make the repair.

After the surgery, they placed him in an induced coma. I was told to watch him. He was sedated but it was crucial that he did not move.

I stayed in his room at the Children's Hospital and there was a little boy in the adjoining room of intensive care. He could not have been more than two years old. He cried all day and all night. I tried to sing to him but it seemed that he was heavily sedated, since he still whimpered day and night. I asked a nurse why this little one was crying and where his parents or relatives were?

She said they just dropped him off for the surgery and were not coming back! When a priest passed by, I asked him about this little one. He said it was very sad and it was true that they did not expect his parents to come back, whether he survived the surgery or not. He said to stay out of it. It was a very delicate situation. He had tried himself to get involved.

I was advised after two days that the doctors were going to give Brandon an injection to remove him from the induced coma and for me to be there. I held his hand to keep him calm. I had been told that patients can hear while they are in a coma.

There was nothing I could do but sing and talk to him. He came out of the coma successfully but complained that his arms were sore and he was in a lot of pain. Evidently they had secured his arms above his head during the surgery. The surgery was so long that now he had to have physical therapy for his arms.

I called to be sure Nicole was all right. A friend was staying at our house and trying to keep Nicole to her routine schedule as much as possible. During the next two days that followed, the surgeons came in and advised me what was next.

The little one next to us continued to whimper. Brandon asked, "What is the matter with the little boy? Why is he alone and what happened to him and where is his mother?" I told him what the nurse and the priest told me about how he was left for heart surgery and was abandoned. Brandon was very quiet for a while and then said, "Mom, why don't you adopt him?" I tried to explain that the doctors were not sure he would survive and that the priest said the social workers were called in to handle the case.

Now Brandon was just interested in getting out of the hospital. He was angry, saying the doctors should be accountable for hurting his arm. He wondered if they would ever be okay again. I told him it was a rough ride for his surgery and to thank God that he was all right. They told him he could not play sports. He liked to ride his skateboard and surfboard. These were approved activities. Just no contact sports.

When reviewing those salvaged medical documents, it was noted that his mother was a drug addict and addicted to alcohol as well. He was born with fetal alcohol syndrome and was addicted to heroin. I was told by his doctor that his nose and lips reflected fetal alcohol syndrome. He said one drink would be enough for him to become an alcoholic as well.

After his heart surgery, I became aware that same year that he was already addicted to alcohol. I enrolled him in several Alcoholics Anonymous support groups for minors. He continued being assisted by more counselors, some even came to the house. One was Boys Town. They did not charge us, and I thought them to be the most effective.

When his room was completed the way he wanted it, he was happy. When I first dropped him off to school and met his teacher, (the one with the revealing conversation about him being suicidal), she told me he was having trouble keeping up. She suspected he had learning disabilities and referred me to a group of psychologists in the area who were able to test him. They said he had several issues that could be affecting his inability to concentrate, but one sure impediment was ADHD. I learned about a physician who was going to give a week-long class in the causes of ADHD and would give suggestions for medication and holistic remedies as well. I signed up and I learned a lot.

His pediatrician said it was a good thing that I did not consent to the ADHD medications because Brandon had facial tics and the medicine was thought to make the facial tics permanent. The physician who gave the week-long class stressed nutrition and structured sleep. (Brandon always found it difficult to fall asleep.) I applied as many of their suggestions that I could, as I was into holistic medicine anyway. We moved forward. His teacher recommended that he be placed in special education and, after presenting the medical records, he continued with special education in the public schools. The Catholic schools were not equipped for special education so despite tutoring, he was unable to keep up and was withdrawn from Catholic school. I had been too busy with Brandon's doctors to call India about his uncle's report on the adoption status in India. Two weeks later, the adoption was still in process and I received a letter which arrived from Mother Teresa's convent. It stated that the adoption laws had changed. I would have to travel to India with an adoption agency to continue.

Having no money or any idea who would take care of the two while I was gone, or for how long I would be required to stay there, I had no other option but to resign myself to the news. In the letter she wrote: "I think God would want you to pursue your intent to adopt another child, considering the concern that you mentioned about finding a sister for her." Nicole and I were very disappointed. Brandon did not say much. His adoption was progressing, pending an investigation and approval by the social worker. This was required by adoption law in Florida. I had paid for the social worker's report with Nicole. His uncle paid for Brandon's. The social worker came to inspect the house and to have a private meeting with Brandon. A week later she presented her report that the adoption was not approved! She said Brandon needed a different setting and his adoption could destroy our family!

    I am sure she used all the required guidelines to determine that it was not to be approved. I was told by a Higher Authority, who approved! The one who told me to "Accept this one, Vera," and that was all I needed. I called his uncle's secretary and told her to get another social worker! She did and it was approved after I told Brandon not to talk much, just to say yes or no to the social worker's questions.

    A few months after the adoption was approved, he went missing when I went to pick him up at school. He was surely hurting from being separated from his grandma and cousins. (Grandma died shortly after being admitted to assisted living.) He went missing at night as well. Sometimes I would wake up and find him asleep on the floor in front of my closed bedroom door.

    His bulimic activity continued. Nicole heard him vomiting after meals and told me about it. She was showing a motherly concern for him.

The first few weeks before his adoption was completed, we were at the public beach. Brandon was surfing. The life guard blew his whistle and announced that he would have to get out of the water due to dangerous weather changes. Brandon was upset. He told me he was going to walk to his cousin's house and surf there. I tried to discourage him, but he was determined and started walking with his surfboard north to their house. Nicole ran after him. I stood there and watched Nicole talking to him; he responded as they proceeded walking a long distance down the beach. I was unsure what to do next. Then I saw them from a distance turning around and walking back! Nicole said she talked him out of it! She then announced that she wanted to learn to surf!

I purchased her an inexpensive surfboard and enrolled them both in classes at Island Water Sports near our house. I enjoyed watching them respond to their instructors. Nicole caught on very quickly and was soon riding waves like a pro. I saw Brandon trying to keep up with her on his expensive surfboard. I thought he was impressed with her, and so was I! She was riding some of the difficult waves better than he was.

    She continued to be there for him. I brought him to a doctor for bulimia. The doctor said just to love him and see how that worked before he would prescribe further treatment. I had a conversation with him, when he returned late one night on his bike. I said, "Son, if you are going to run away, please do it in the daylight as I am worrying too much when you do it at night!" I asked him to bring food and sunscreen with him.

    Both children were very fair skinned. I had them both checked out at the Children's Hospital for suspicious growths, which were removed and checked for cancer. The tests came back negative. I was told with both present, that they would have to use sunscreen every day, especially living in Florida. They advised the exposure to be the most harmful between 12 p.m. and 3 p.m. and were to be avoided. They both used their sunscreen and tried to conform to the doctor's orders.

    Because of my novel request about worrying about Brandon running away at night,

Brandon relented. He would become very emotional and angry at times. I brought him to several counselors, some weekly. When I would observe the first sign of agitation or his stressing, I would ask him if he wanted me to rock him in my grandmother's rocking chair. It was sent to me from Philadelphia after Grandmother died. I used it when Nicole was born. I was surprised when he consented! He was so small. He fit on my lap at ten years old! I had composed a lullaby for Nicole and did the same for each child.

Brandon required a lot of treatment with psychologists and psychiatrists. I must say the rocking chair worked the best! His episodes of depression seemed to be getting fewer. Brandon had never been baptized in the Catholic Church even though his family was Catholic. Immediately after the adoption was completed, I arranged for his Baptism and First Communion—all in one. I had a party to follow. Brandon had to attend classes for those two sacraments and liked the nuns at the church who were treating him so kindly. After the ceremony Brandon said, "Mom, I cannot believe I never heard about Jesus." He was smiling a lot more now.

    I joined a local charismatic Catholic church and proceeded to bring the two of them there. They were in Christmas pageants, plays, and other activities. Nicole learned liturgical dance. The pastor was getting a new set of drums for the choir and asked Brandon, who was always hanging out watching the drummer play, if he would like the old set. Brandon said yes and the drummer became his instructor for two years, and was later his confirmation sponsor. The drum instructor taught Brandon to read music. He then wanted to learn piano, and in no time he was playing mine. He had a children's recital at the nearby university. He did well. He did not use his sheet music on the concert piano on stage. He did better than I did at Miami University!

    One Lenten season, the church had an imprinted cloth over the cross. The cloth covered the entire cross and was imprinted with the crucified Christ's face. The church also had large copies of it printed on posters and they were for sale. I purchased several and mounted one on the hallway wall next to his bedroom.

He could see it with his bedroom door open, while lying in his bed.

He told me that when he was feeling sad, he would look at the picture, and Christ would wink at him! This happened several times. I told him I was sure Jesus did wink at him and was so happy that His little brother, Brandon, was safe at last and learning more about Him! When Brandon left home at 18 years old, he brought the picture with him. If it got lost or damaged he would request another copy.

After the adoption and the Baptism were completed, I decided that we would all travel every weekend to River Ranch, which was about a two hour drive north of us. They had cabins and rooms for rent with kitchenettes. Every Friday they had a rodeo and during the day there was horseback riding, boating on the river, and a luxurious pool and spa area. We would bring food and prepare some meals.

They had a cafe as well. River Ranch was a very large operation. They had a security guard who could fly in with his aircraft and land at the ranch. They had lots of animals similar to a small zoo. We were allowed to gather eggs from the chickens and the two children thought this was great. Brandon did not like horseback riding much but Nicole was in heaven, always asking for the same horse to ride. I thought this would be a good way for them to bond. I was concerned about their bonding. Brandon tried horseback riding with Nicole at the ranch until her horse, who was following behind Brandon, bit the rear end of Brandon's horse!

The horse took off, giving Brandon a hair-raising ride. He was not at all interested in riding horses after that experience. He did like hanging out in the heated spa and also liked playing pool at the clubhouse. They both enjoyed the rodeo every Friday night and it was always preceded by a country barbecue with country music. Nicole found other girls that liked to ride and some had their own horses. We did this for a year and a half. Since we had no family nearby, we even spent Christmas and Thanksgiving at River Ranch. They had an old, historic Catholic church nearby and the children received a lot of attention from the church community, who were mostly the workers from the orange groves nearby. They worked for a well-known plant that produced Florida's orange juice. We were invited to their traditional sunrise Easter service at a shrine in the woods. We had to arrive before dawn. When the sun came up, hovering over the altar at the shrine, it was breathtaking! I thought this was a wonderful way to spend Easter morning. After the Easter Mass was completed at the shrine, we went across the street to a very good family restaurant for breakfast. I was surprised that so many families were up that early.

Thanksgiving at River Ranch offered so many choices for family participation. There were elaborate hayrides, skeet shooting, fishing, barbecues, boat rides on the river, and other surprise holiday events. The children participated and enjoyed them all. At the rural Catholic church, near River Ranch, the parishioners continued with their interest in the two children, welcoming them before and after the service.

I was satisfied that the children's bonding was successful and I had fun watching it.

Brandon at local university recital

Brandon and Nicole sliding down
the hill at new house

Picture that Brandon said winked at him and that he brought with him when he left home

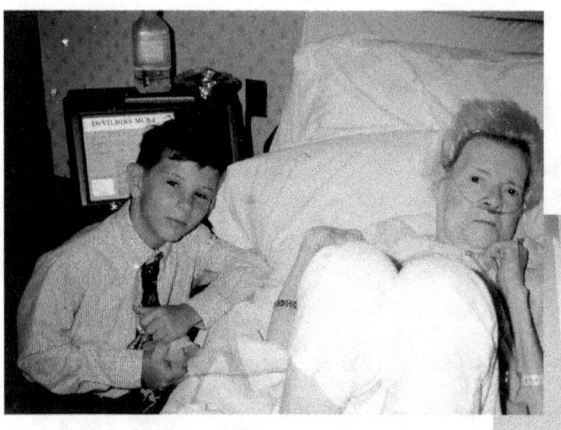

Brandon and his grandmother at the hospital

Brandon painting his room

Brandon on horse at River Ranch

MISSIONARIES OF CHARITY
NIRMALA SHISHU BHAVAN
78, A.J.C. BOSE ROAD
CALCUTTA 14

29 Nov 1996

Dear Vera,

    Our dear Mother is very ill in hospital at this moment. I am sure that you are holding her in your prayers at this time.

    We do not have a procedure set up to do adoptions in the U.S. at this time.

    Your story is an inspiring one and your faith quite beautiful. We wish we could help you but are unable.

    If your heart is telling you to take this action then you must, and if you have found a reputable agency who will guarantee you are very fortunate.

    We will pray for you in your search to give yourself and Nicole more love with another child.

    God bless you

               Sr. Marjorie m.c.

Mother Teresa letter regarding adoption

CHAPTER 10

Grandpa Peter

Brandon was benefiting from the single parents ministry as well. I remember his first pumpkin carving event with the children of the single parents group. I took pictures of Nicole and Brandon carving the pumpkins together. They were smiling.

We then acquired an English rabbit, which we named Mr. Emily. (We did not realize at the time that he was a mister and not a miss.) Nicole had chosen our first dog, Roxie, a lab mix, from an animal rescue. Roxie was very intelligent and well-behaved. We would go to the local nursing homes and assisted-living facilities in the area on holidays. We had permission to bring both pets. For Thanksgiving, Brandon was dressed as a turkey, with an authentic turkey nose I found for him.

Nicole wore her angel wings. I would dress as a pilgrim or sometimes an Indian. We would bring balloons and treats and, of course, the two pets. Mr. Emily was very loving with the seniors and so was Roxie, who was trained to kiss the hand of a senior on command. We would ask the seniors if they wanted a kiss from Roxie. If they said yes, we told them to extend their hand and commanded Roxie to give kisses to grandma or grandpa, pointing to their extended hand. Roxie never missed one senior!

Mr. Emily the English rabbit was very intelligent. It was amazing that a rabbit was able to learn tricks as well! It was a total delight to the seniors, who were not prepared for a rabbit who could learn tricks. One lady of 100 years asked if she could purchase Roxie, as she missed her pet so much. She asked if Roxie could climb up onto her bed and give her kisses!

After we received initial approvals from several facilities, it became a tradition on Thanksgiving and Christmas to expect the Verna Children. At one nursing home, which turned out to be our last stop, the children and I were asked to join the seniors for Thanksgiving dinner! Some of the assisted-living facilities would ask us over the following years to present the children and our pets, and would gather those seniors in a large community hall for a show! Even a local church heard about our performances, and an article appeared on the first page of the local Catholic newspaper with pictures and articles written by their editor who had been attending the event and interviewing the seniors.

For our Christmas presentation, we had the same routine. This time, Brandon was dressed in an authentic Santa Claus outfit. Both Nicole and I, with angel wings, would sing Christmas carols. Brandon made it part of his Thanksgiving routine to ask the seniors what they wanted for Christmas. He would bring a pad and pen to write down their names and room number. They would ask for little things like powder, hair nets, brushes, and mostly toiletries for both the men and the women. For Christmas we would bring teddy bears as a surprise gift for many who wanted them. The extras were stored for the following Christmas. Surprisingly, very few seniors declined the teddy bears. Then Brandon, now dressed in his Santa suit, would give each one what they requested!

We brought enough teddy bears so that no one would be without a Christmas gift.

One Thanksgiving, we were proceeding with our routine in a nursing home trying not to miss any of the rooms — since most were unable to gather in their community room for the pet show. Most were bedridden or seated in wheelchairs outside their room. I asked the director if we missed any seniors. She said there was another room in the rear where several seniors were in wheelchairs and on oxygen. Everyone was smiling when we entered. I spotted one elderly woman enjoying all this from the back of the room. She was on oxygen and watching us intently. I went over to her and told her that Brandon, the Turkey Man, was taking orders for Christmas and I could tell him what she would like. She seemed just happy to watch and could not speak well with her oxygen mask.

The following Sunday we were attending Mass at a close-by, small church that we seldom attended (since we always preferred our charismatic Catholic church). As we were standing outside, a gentlemen approached us and said: "You were the ones last week at the nursing home. I passed you as you were leaving in your outfits and was told of your activities every year." He said he had just placed his wife there and was told by the nurses that besides himself, we three were the last to see her alive!

He said she died from loss of oxygen that night. He thanked us for going there, dressed up in our Thanksgiving costumes. He said they had seven children and she missed them, but she sure she enjoyed our visit. He introduced himself as Peter and told us that they had been married for 50 years and that they met in the Army. She was a nurse. He was wearing an oxygen mask, too! He said they smoked heavily and his wife had just nursed him through lung cancer surgery. He had huge scars on his neck. It looked like they had to remove a lot of tissue to get it all. He seemed very distraught because he was told he was not expected to survive, and it was his dear wife's nursing that he survived, and now she did not! Brandon and Nicole were listening to the entire conversation and said: "Mommy, ask him to go with us to breakfast." We did go to breakfast and began to see him a lot, as he lived close by.

Peter told me that he needed eye surgery. I asked him if I could accompany him to the surgery, as he was nervous since he was on oxygen. I told him I would pick him up early and stay with him for the surgery. I would be there when he recovered and would bring him something to eat afterwards. I held his hand before he went under and we said a prayer together. The doctor came over, thinking I was family and told me it went well but that he was more concerned about his heart condition. I asked Peter later if I could accompany him to his next heart appointment. He consented. He could not eat and talk at the same time and it was very noticeable. The children would ask me, "What happened to Peter?" He invited us out often and we became very close. The two children called him Grandpa Peter and had become attached to him and his doting.

Peter's children and grandchildren were scattered in different states up north. He had a daughter who was a nurse living a short distance from him, but she was always busy with her new doctor friend and rarely available for him. When I brought Peter to his cardiologist, he said he will be okay as long as he is on oxygen 24/7. He said his surgeries and the sudden death of his wife had taken a lot out of him.

I found out that I had to go to Cleveland Clinic hospital myself for a week of observation for my heart! Grandpa Peter said, "Just bring the two children to my house. I will take care of them while you are in the hospital." Since he literally raised his own seven children, I was confident that he knew what to do and I was relieved to know that the children would be safe. I left their favorite food and clothes for school with Peter. He had a car and could drive them to their school right around the corner.

His daily routine was to sit in his easy chair and watch EWTN, a Catholic channel I was not yet familiar with. He could fall asleep in an upright position on his leather chair and it proved better for his breathing. He had been an officer in the Army and was used to taking over no matter what the situation demanded. When I returned, the children said Grandpa Peter had spoiled them. They were in no hurry to leave. He was a daily Mass goer; we would meet for Mass after I dropped off the two children in the same Catholic school nearby. We would sit in the back of the church, because his oxygen machine made a lot of noise and he did not want to disturb anyone.

We would go to his favorite breakfast place. After a week, the waitress said, "Well, who is this young lady you are having breakfast with every day?" He answered, "This is my daughter, Vera Marie." He truly had become Dad to me. I thanked God for Grandpa Peter. Several years later, his eldest son came to town and told him they were selling his house. He had given his eldest power of attorney, who was very firm about Peter moving back to North Jersey, where his son lived. Peter had another property which he and his wife had purchased in another state. The Florida home sold quickly. I was still going over to see him every day to keep to our former routine as much as possible.

The last garage sale left him with a few items that no one wanted, including a very large rooster collection and two mahogany shelves—which he made himself—that could be mounted on the wall. I absolutely loved roosters and asked if I could purchase his extensive collection. Also, the two custom-made, wood shelves would be perfect for my small, antique items.

He said, "Pay for them? No chance! I am just delighted that you will have them." He said, "Take the green-leather easy chair, too. No one wanted it." I gave him a big hug and thanked him. He said he sold his car and noted that I needed a new car, but his old one was not worth fixing. He said, "Take this $5,000 and put it toward a new car. I would put you and the children in my will, but my family would contest it." I was devastated that I would lose my Dad. I asked him to come live with us! Why go back to New Jersey and live alone? None of his children offered him a place. He said he would love to do just that! He told me that he had a hernia that was bothering him a lot and he did not want to burden me with it. He would have it taken care of when he arrived in New Jersey.

I told him that I would put our small house up for sale and would purchase a larger one. I would plan to have oxygen installed in his bedroom. We parted, happy to know that we would see each other again soon. A few days after he left, I was looking for time to put the house on the market and considering which areas to search for a large home that would be affordable, when a car pulled in front of my house. I was standing out front walking Mr. Emily. I had dropped off the children at school and, before heading to work, I wanted to walk Mr. Emily, who I refused to keep in a cage. He used a litter box. I thought I'd walk him outside for fresh air. We did not have Nicole's dog Roxie yet. A man got out of his car and stared at me with Mr. Emily for a moment. He stated: "I need to buy your house!" I thought: Well, how did he know it was even for sale? I had no sign and no chance to talk to anyone about it, not even the children.

The man identified himself and said his son just purchased a house behind me. My fence was on the shared property line. The son's house was directly behind mine, but his front faced the next street over. He said his son was single, and when he found out his father had a terminal illness, purchased a large house so that he could take care of his mother.

The man said he did not feel comfortable with his wife having to move in with him and would prefer her to have her own little house. He did not ask to see inside but said he would pay cash for it. I told him I had just decided to put the house on the market but did not get a chance to research larger homes in the area. I said I researched what a two bedroom that was improved would sell for and I planned to put it up for $150,000. He said he would pay cash for it immediately and did not even ask to see it!

 I said, "Great, but I have to research and would have to look first to see what houses were for sale." He asked if I had seen the four bedroom house with a den up the hill. He viewed it and said it was just listed with a realtor for $150,000. He thought it was too large for his wife, and mine would be more convenient. His son would be able to put a gate in my fence, which was on the property line, and have access to his wife without having to drive around the block to check on her.

 He said, "Go and take a look and let me know," and gave me his phone number. I put Mr. Emily back in the house and drove up the hill to see the house that was just listed, and retrieved the realtor's phone number off the sign that had been installed that morning. I made an appointment with the realtor to see it at 12 p.m. She said the nurse, who was the owner, would be there as well.

    I stood out front looking at the house's elevation and thought to myself that there was nothing I could do to improve it. I had worked with so many builders and they would suggest certain elevation improvements. There seemed to be no way to make improvements! It had to be the ugliest I had ever encountered!

    My little, all-white cottage had a nice Key West style elevation. It appeared larger, with white tiles throughout the house, and had a single car garage. This house did not have a garage, but a makeshift carport. I couldn't change the weird pillars that were supporting the roof, and the windows were roll-out instead of the more modern windows in my house.

    I showed up on time for the appointment and the owner and her realtor showed me around. The floors were all brown tile. The kitchen was the only updated room and it was dark brown. The three bedrooms were average. The master bedroom was larger than most. I was told the owners built it themselves. The master bathroom was ridiculous. It was so small that a couple would not be able to occupy it together. A single user would have trouble as well and more so if he or she was overweight! The single vanity and sink were very small. I wondered who was the architect who designed this house. The wife, who was a nurse, told me that her husband had just passed away and her older son found his own place. She said she and her husband built the house and later put an addition on the south side to create a larger master, but to modify the master bath would have been too expensive.

I asked why the master bedroom had a window air conditioner. She said the add-on to the master bedroom would be more than the central air unit could handle. Well I thought, what a mess! The realtor said it was a double lot and located on a high coral ridge. No flood insurance would be required, even though it was a mile from the ocean. I thought to myself, "Well, it is a great location and it's certainly large enough." I liked the formal library off the entrance! I told the realtor I would take it and pay cash, since I had a cash offer to purchase mine. I brought a blank contract with me (as was my practice to do so), and proceeded to fill it out. We both signed it for closing within 30 days! The owner was happy and offered me a large church bench if I wanted it, as she was downsizing and had no room for it. I liked it and thanked her for it. I have still have it 30 years later. I called Grandpa Peter and told him I sold my current house and purchased a large house that would be closing in 30 days.

We closed my little house first and I was able to deliver the cash for the second closing. I called Grandpa Peter to tell him we closed. He was so happy, but he was still in the hospital. I told him I would put oxygen in the front room.

A week after closing, we were settled in. We did not need movers, as the two children thought it was a novel idea to just bring their things themselves up the hill. We used the station wagon for trips and brought the mattresses, strapped onto the roof. They thought this was a great idea and I am sure the neighbors did as well! Brandon was creative and helped orchestrate the move.

They both chose a color and painted their bedrooms. They did a really good job. The back of the house sloped down, as the elevation of the house was high. I decided to get a large tarp and set it up so that they could slide down after wetting it with a long hose. It was a great way to cool off. I was surprised that Brandon enjoyed it as much as she did. I immediately called Grandpa and told him everything. He said he thought he would be discharged very soon and would keep me posted every day. When he was finally discharged from the hospital, he was still struggling with his breathing and was on standby with the hospital doctors, as they had not removed his stitches or released him. He called afterward to tell me he was officially released and that his children had put him in a duplex-like building temporarily, as he said he was leaving for Florida.

 He had one window air conditioner and they hired a nurse to help him. It had one set of burners for cooking. He sent me a picture of it with him standing out front. I thought I should immediately fly up to bring him back! He said he was booking a flight and not to worry. The next day, I received a call that he had died that night. The air conditioner was not working. They said he died from loss of oxygen! It was summertime and I could not imagine having no air conditioning. I called and made reservations for myself and the children to attend the wake and the funeral at his hometown church in North New Jersey. I booked hotel reservations nearby and ordered a rental car that would be picked up at the airport. All three of us were having a difficult time trying to adjust to what had happened to Grandpa since all the changes were made so quickly for him to come to live with us.

When we arrived for the funeral, the priest announced that Vera, Nicole, and Brandon had arrived and asked us to stand up. He said that he was able to visit Peter every day at the hospital and even at the duplex. He said Peter was so happy that he was moving to be with his beloved family in Florida and he could not wait to travel to be with them. The church was full and everyone turned to look at us. The children did not know how to react and were trying to process his death.

The night before was the wake. Peter was laid out in his Army uniform. His sisters came up to me and told me that Peter had lost twins when his wife miscarried, and mourned their loss for a lot of years. They said he would be happy now in heaven with them and his wife, who they said he adored and had helped her with everything he could with raising seven children. I had never heard that story and wondered where his sisters were when he needed them.

Grandpa Peter

Martin Destefano, 95, a resident of Avante nursing home in Boca Raton, enjoys Mr. Emily's visit.

Lillian Greenhouse, 97, shakes Mr. Emily's paw. Greenhouse is also a resident of Avante nursing home in Boca Raton.

FLORIDA CATHOLIC PHOTOS BY LINDA REEVES

Vera Marie Verna hopes to build on the success of her rabbit ministry and establish a care facility for mothers, children and seniors.

VERNA: Family uses rabbits and a dog to lift up spirits of nursing home residents

FROM A1

troops — 20 to 30 children from the two parishes — for three big events each year: Easter, Thanksgiving and Christmas.

Her own three adopted children, Brandon, 21, Nicole, 16, and Peter, 7, also join their mother in her ministry. The three dress up on the holiday visits as Pilgrims, Indians, angels and Santa.

"I believe in the power of intergenerational kindness and need," Verna said. "The faces of the elderly turn to joy, smiles wreathing their faces. They love the children and remember them from one year to the next. And of course they remember the rabbits and the rabbits' pet, Roxie the lab."

Verna said Mr. Emily, herself a senior citizen in rabbit years, has a special talent that delights those they visit.

"She has the ability to memorize names," she said. "We introduce each person to the rabbit, then we move that person to the other side of the room. When we ask Mr. Emily, 'Where is Brian?' for example, the rabbit will turn around and point to Brian with her head. That amazes and astonishes everyone in the room."

The director of Avante nursing home in Boca Raton, one of the facilities Verna visits with her clan, is pleased that she comes with her children and animals.

"The animals are a wonderful concept," said Kim Simmons, administrator. "Rabbits are great

they are gentle. We hope to expand on the idea one day and have animals roaming in the halls and rooms. The people love them and the animals help patients who are experiencing depression."

The residents are pleased, too, about the four-legged friends visiting their housing facilities.

"I love animals," said Lillian Greenhouse, 97, who will celebrate her birthday Feb. 1. "I used to have a dog. I love rabbits."

"The rabbit is soft and really cute," said Martin Destefano, in his 90s. "I love to pet animals."

Verna said the residents fall in love with the friendly, furry animals and especially enjoy kisses from Roxie and hugs from the children.

"I had one lady ask me how much I would take for Mr. Emily," said Verna. "She wanted to buy her."

Verna hopes to expand her outreach one day. Her vision is to provide a care facility dedicated to serving people of all faiths and ages — a facility for children, seniors and poor women in crisis.

"We will not worry about where they come from or who they are. We will care for everyone in need, showing them the love of Christ," she said.

Ministry to nursing homes and assisted living

Ministry to nursing homes and assisted living

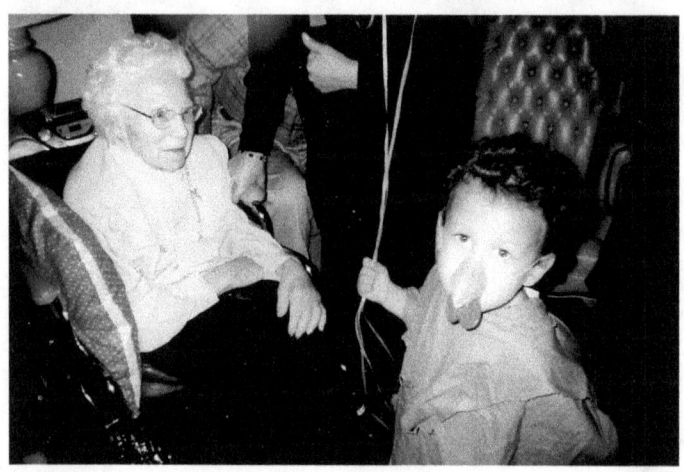

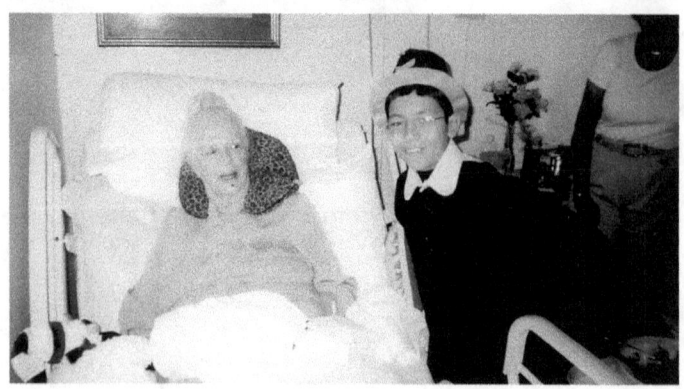

CHAPTER 11

Third Adoption/Mother Teresa/ The Carmelites

The two children were enjoying their large bedrooms as much as I was enjoying the formal library. Nine months after we moved in, the adoption attorney for the first adoption was now my next door neighbor. When we moved in, she asked me if I wanted to adopt more children now that I had a larger house. I said absolutely not! Not at age 56! I recited an old nursery rhyme to her. "There was an old lady that lived in a shoe, she had so many children she did not know what to do." I had my hands full!

One morning at about 7:30 a.m., she knocked on my front door. I told her that I was getting ready to drop the children off at school and then rush to the morning Mass at a nearby church. I asked if I could call her afterwards.

I was late for the service, and the homily was in progress. As I was scrambling to find a seat, I heard the priest, who was speaking about the need to evangelize, say, "Yes, even when you adopt a child, it's like going to the mission field!" I stopped cold and thought. Oh, no! The attorney wants me to adopt again. I thought it was unusual that she would come over that early. I waited until everyone left the chapel. Sitting alone, I spoke to Our Father. "Father, I think the attorney wants me to adopt again. I don't think I can handle another one. The two you sent had so many medical issues. I am totally bankrupt. I have Grandpa Peter's $5,000 that he gave me before he died and that's it, no savings or other cash. I have $2,000 in my checking account. I am 56 years old, soon to be 57. How will I be able to adopt another one?"

He said, "Yes, she will be asking you to adopt another infant. If you say no, I won't be upset with you. I know it is a lot to ask of you and it will be difficult, but would you take the child for Me?" I could not say no to my kind and loving Father. I responded, "I will take the child." I remember all these years what He said next: "It will be okay. Just show them who I am and I will do the rest!" So many times during their teen years, I reminded Him of that promise and He took care of them every time!

When I arrived back home, I called the attorney at her office. I said, "I know you are going to ask me to adopt another child." She said, "How did you know?" I said, "Well you are, right?" She said, "Yes. The birth mother of Nicole has a terminal illness now and is pregnant again. She called to ask if you would take the one to be born soon. She is putting this one up to be adopted as well. They would be siblings (although with different fathers). We don't know if it's a boy or girl, once again the sonogram could not identify the sex due to the position of the infant in the womb." I told her I had little money now, only $7,000. She said she would work with me. I had a closing coming up for Verna Realty and would have my commission to contribute. Since the infant was to be born soon, she said she could make it work with fewer expenses. Two months later, Holy Cross Hospital called to tell me it was a boy and that he was premature and also experienced a difficult birth.

The attorney was out of town and gave permission for the two children and myself to go to the hospital to see him. We had to suit up and wear masks, as he was in an incubator. When we arrived, he was screaming and not drinking the bottle that was propped up in the incubator. The mother had left the hospital. I asked the nurse to take him out of the incubator and to bring me another bottle of formula so I could feed him. She did and he stopped crying.

He was very underweight, with long skinny legs. He listened very intently to what I was saying and began to drink his new bottle. His brother and sister spoke to him, saying, "Don't cry, little brother. It will be all right. Don't be afraid. We will be coming back for you." He drank the entire bottle and they put him back into the incubator. We were asked to leave and waited outside the door to be sure he would not start to cry again. He was okay. I asked the nurses when we could take him home. She said, "Soon, since it is obvious that he wants to be held to drink his nourishment." She said, "You can do that for him since he is underweight and needs around the clock care. We will tell you how many times a day you will need to feed him and give him his medication."

I asked her to order a case of the same formula they were using and I would pay for it.
   I was soon ready with clothes, diapers, and a crib. The master bedroom was so large. I asked a friend to divide the room with two French doors (glass panels) to create a nursery. It had been completed weeks before and worked out well. I moved my desk to the library so there would be room for his crib and the changing table next to his bed. We picked out a Peter Rabbit theme to decorate his room.
   The two children had been working on a name prior to his birth. They were talking about Maxine if it is a girl and Maxwell if it was a boy. Since we used Grandpa Peter's $5,000 toward the adoption, I thought his name should be Peter Maxwell. They agreed. The rabbit theme for his room was right on. Grandpa would be so happy. I knew he was watching from above. He told me that none of his children were given the name Peter.
   When the adoption was finalized, we had an impromptu Baptism at the charismatic church. I was told there would be no room at the church for an after party, so I planned a tailgate party in the parking lot and set it up

behind the Volvo station wagon. I brought a few folding chairs, food, drinks, and white paper goods to serve the food. The priest was invited and gave a blessing over the food.

His godparents, who had agreed to take the required baptismal instruction at the church, brought their daughter (who had become a friend to Nicole) and their son (who was a friend to Brandon). I brought white tablecloths and white flowers. I put flowers on the altar and decorated the tailgate with them as well. No one was in a hurry to leave, even the priest stayed for the reception. I brought a bubbly fruit drink and served it in plastic champagne glasses that were tied with white ribbon, to toast his Baptism.

Since I was still a single mom, I made sure that all three children received religious education and would learn about their Father in heaven. I told the children that they were adopted by a single mother. Unfortunately they had no earthly father. I emphasized that they indeed had the best Father, our heavenly Father, our God, the Mighty One. Each Father's Day we would celebrate by sending up balloons with handwritten notes from each of them attached, wishing Our Father in heaven a happy Father's Day. It became an ongoing tradition to this day, 35 years later. Every Father's Day we would gather and many asked to join us for the ongoing tradition at our home. Afterwards we attended Father's Day Mass on Sunday at our church. We would gather outside our house to launch the balloons.

Everyone enjoyed brunch together. Over the years, we had more than twenty people attend this tradition. One woman came in her wheelchair! When Peter was four years old, the mother of two little boys that Peter met at a birthday party invited him to swim and play at their mansion's pool. The mother picked up Peter and assured me they would be well supervised and that she would drop him back in a few hours. The boys liked Peter and so did their parents. One Saturday their father called and said that he and his wife were taking their sons with them to lunch at their country club. The father, who I had never met, said to have Peter ready. He promised that Peter would return no later than 3:30 p.m. The parents showed up with their two little boys in the back seat of their car. I walked Peter out to the car and the father rolled down the window and introduced himself, saying that his sons had requested Peter's company and that they would be well supervised. I helped Peter into the back seat between the two little boys. Right on time, Peter returned by 3:30 p.m. I was told he behaved well and that they had fun. The next morning I received a call from the father.

He wanted to give me condolences on the death of Peter's father. (He and his wife did not know that Peter was adopted.) I told him that Peter was adopted by me! Why was he offering me condolences on the death of my husband? He said when we picked up Peter yesterday, he asked him, "So, Peter, that's your mother, so where is your father?" He said Peter responded without hesitation, "He is in heaven." He said he wanted to give his condolences and asked when his father died. I told him about our tradition with the balloons and how all three of my adopted children had come to know that they had a loving father in heaven, Father God! The man was silent for a few moments and then said, "Oh okay, I see," and hung up! I smiled to myself and thought that our great Father in heaven must have enjoyed Peter's comment! I asked: "So Father, did I do what you asked of me when you said, 'Just show them who I am and I will do the rest?'"

In elementary school, Peter's teachers, especially the school principal, praised him on every level. He received every kind of award. He was very kind to everyone and polite even to the ones who wanted to fight and tried to rouse him constantly. He was the tallest and strongest of all the children in elementary school. I enrolled him at the YMCA for every sport they offered. Golfing was not offered, but I took him to the public course. He excelled in every sport. His coaches would tell me that he was a true athlete. His favorite was basketball and he played with the local leagues well into middle school.

In public middle school, everyone had a phone. He wanted one as well. I agreed, but thought I would start with my own phone to lend him during the day so that I could keep an eye on his activity. Was I ever surprised! The conversations and photos that were sent to him were so outrageous that I brought it to the attention of the middle school principal. The principal said it was normal! Nothing was at all wrong with the hookups and the pictures that bordered on pornography! He commented that even the profane language of the senders was completely normal. Well, it wasn't in my opinion. Just before the school year ended, I applied to Catholic middle school. It was very pricey, but I was told I could be eligible for a scholarship because of Peter's excellent grades and my low income. I was told to hurry with the application, as the grade was filling up fast with returning students and would be at full capacity very soon! I rushed to complete it.

The school said I did it in record time and he was accepted! I received the tuition modifications and ordered his uniforms. The first week of school was an adjustment for Peter because of the uniforms and, as he said, "All that praying!" The second week, I was advised that there would be a special music prayer service for parents right after school in the adjoining church. The musicians and the choir were church members. I had never been to their church and thought I should attend with the other parents. I asked Peter to come along since school was out and there were no aftercare classrooms yet. He decided to come along and wait for me in the church. He sat off to the side alone but still had a good view of the band and the choir. It appeared to me that he was actually enjoying the music. He looked intrigued and focused on one of the lead guitar players, who was one of the youngest musicians in the group.

After the service, he came over to me and said, "Follow me, I want you to speak to that guitar player." He went up to him and said, "Here, talk to my mom about lessons. I want to play with you, too!" The guitarist told me which kind of starter guitar to look for and the best place to purchase one. He also told me that he would be available to give Peter lessons. He did for two years. I was surprised and pleased that he was now enjoying middle school. He joined the basketball team and became an assistant to the coach. He helped the coach with the girls and boys on the middle school teams and continued to do so for the remaining years at middle school. The principal told me that he was being called "the silent giant" (he was over six feet tall and was a young man of few words). She said she observed and admired how he handled himself and acclimated to the others. Just like in elementary school, he promoted peace among the other students. She made sure he received the tuition assistance until he graduated and also recommended him to the Catholic high school for it. He was able to receive it for all four years. The principal continued to help each year with other fees and books. We joined the church and she would ask the pastor to approve the payment of his out-of-pocket fees and support for his basketball fees. He continued with basketball for all four years of high school. He enjoyed traveling with the team to tournaments.

He also joined a city basketball team in the next town and traveled to tournaments with them as well. The middle school years went by quickly. After dropping him off at school, I would go to the 8 a.m. Mass as our family was now registered parishioners at this Carmelite church. One weekday, a Carmelite priest invited anyone who desired to pray the Liturgy of the Hours after Mass. He said devotion leads to Jesus and that we should obey the words of

Mary, His Mother. "Do whatever he tells you" (John 2:5).

Their primary charism was a pledge of allegiance to Jesus Christ and that it would be a serious error to do otherwise! It took the form of the mission of Christ to tell of the nearness of God's love and to celebrate the inestimable worth of every human being! I had arrived on that same page! For seven years, that saintly Carmelite priest who answered all my questions said, "Why don't you check out joining the Carmelite order at a nearby church?" He gave me the phone number and who to contact. I did and was very impressed with their community. They treated everyone in their community group with love and concern and reinforced that we were all brothers and sisters in the group. They went out of their way to make me feel that I was home at last!

I had been volunteering to help the Mother Teresa nuns at their convent in Miami off and on for many years. I would go there early in the morning on weekends for Mass at their convent across the street from the large soup kitchen that they operated. I so loved and admired Mother Teresa and was thinking about joining their lay order. Sometimes I would stay overnight on Fridays at a motel and be there at dawn to assist with the soup kitchen. Some 600 meals were served a day, mostly serving the poor and homeless.

Mass at the convent was always a treat. I would try to keep up with them (as the nuns always sat on the floor), getting up and down until the Mother Superior one Saturday just went and found me a chair. She told me to just use the chair. "You are not used to sitting and kneeling on the floor!" I would then walk across the street and help with the soup kitchen duties.

The convent provided outdoor showers for the homeless men to wash up in a secluded area. They would then be seated at these long narrow tables to be served lunch. Volunteers would then put on our aprons and help serve the food to each man (over 80 were served at the sit-down lunch). One of the nuns would lead them in saying a prayer in two languages, English and Spanish, thanking God for their food. I was so impressed with how quiet and respectful these men were to each other and the servers. I would also help with the food distribution to the women and their children. Hundreds of sandwiches were given out as well as bags of fresh fruit and cooked food if they wanted it. All of it was put in their to-go bags. Sometimes I would help cook the to-go food. The nuns would say that this was probably the only meal they would have for the day or sometimes the week.

One Saturday, the Mother Superior told me to stay after Mass to speak with me. I had been asking a lot of questions about joining the lay order. She began by saying: "Our ministry is always in dangerous areas of Miami and our soup kitchen no exception. That is why I always tell you not to park your car on the street but behind the tall iron gates in the courtyard and to lock the gate behind you. Our mission also brings us to the poorer neighborhoods to visit seniors on a regular basis. We service a lot of seniors and poor families, most in the late afternoons. We clean their houses or apartments and bring food to them on a routine basis. You belong home with your children, especially on the weekends and on these late afternoon visits. I don't think this work is for you right now." (I had not adopted Peter yet.)

After watching Mother Teresa's original movie, I had a great love for her and her work. I knew Mother Superior had a good point and I went across the street to say my goodbyes. I did not know that the soup kitchen had a second floor. I was told that some of the volunteers might be up there. When I went upstairs, I was confronted with a most beautiful chapel. It had a relic of Mother Teresa there in front of the altar. I prayed and told Mother Teresa that the Mother Superior was right about her evaluation. How would I be able to serve now as she did?!

As I was leaving, I noticed a large room off to the left. I walked in and was startled to find the room full of baby cribs and small cots beside the cribs. The cribs and cots were neatly made up. It was a Saturday and no one was there. Baby clothing and other items were on shelves. I was stunned! This is what I wanted to do. I had been trying to build maternity houses for years now to take the mothers into my home and provide assistance as needed for their deliveries. So, the nuns here in Miami were doing it above the soup kitchen! I went back downstairs and found Mother Superior and told her she was so right about her assessment. I knew now how I could serve as Mother Teresa did at her orphanage: housing the mothers and their children and placing their children for adoption, if the mothers could not take care of their babies. I thanked her and continued pursuit to present.

I knew I had to find a way to feed the pregnant lambs and their babies and also the senior lambs! After many contracts on many properties and applying for HUD loans, none were successful for one reason or another. Even though the HUD loans were approved after I paid the filing fee, they fell apart. I knew I had to just persevere.

I met with the group that the Carmelite priest recommended. I was very happy to find that they were on the same page that I was. Their charism was contemplative prayer, service to others, and community. To their own community as well. The members of the third order of Carmelites were very welcoming and told me each Carmelite community was a family of brothers and sisters of Carmel. I was assigned a wonderful Carmelite to be my formation director.

I asked so many more questions of her that first year, which she answered. I am fortunate that the same formation director continues to answer all my questions with her help and example. Along with my other brothers and sister Carmelites, I have learned what it means to just be still and quiet and listen to what the Lord is saying, thanks to their instruction and teaching of what contemplative prayer was all about. I was learning to be open to whatever God had to say about the direction my journey would take. I learned not to jump ahead of Him but to wait for His will and not mine to be done. I was able to find out what God had to say about my desire to continue my journey of service.

My accomplishment this year was securing a trademark/service mark for intergenerational care for the state of Florida, which was a result of His doing, not mine! I am more patient and willing to wait for his timing. Just as I had to wait until the ages of 47 to 57 to adopt the children that he offered me without my soliciting them. I devour the Liturgy of the Hours readings every day. I thank Him for this privilege to be part of the Carmelite charism.

"Happy Father's Day God" picture altered by Brandon celebrating Father's Day for over 20 years

Two little boyfriends, when their father asked Peter, "Where is your father?" Peter answering: "In heaven!"

Hospital with premature baby Peter

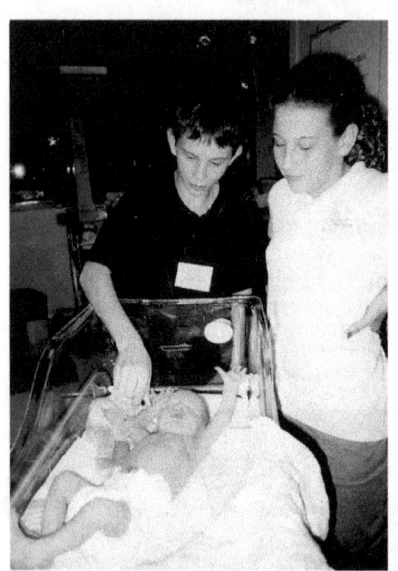
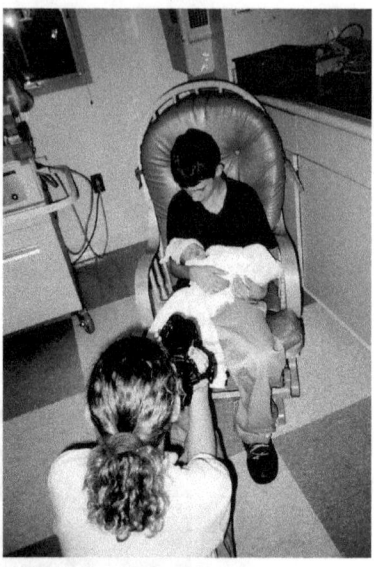
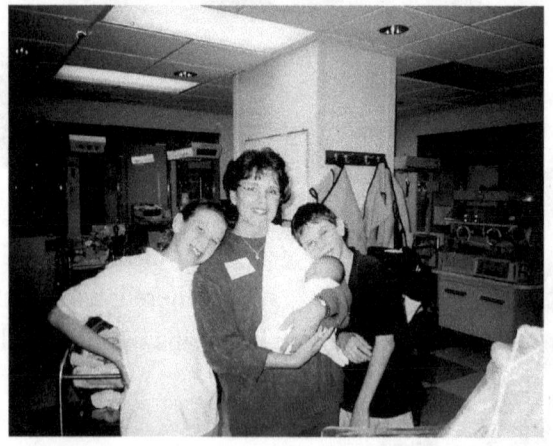

CHAPTER 12

Journey Update 30 Years Later/ Feeding Pregnant and Senior Lambs

For the last 30 years and since the first adoption, my old friends (pre-adoption friends), I called them my "BC" (before children) friends, would ask me, "Why are you so joyful and happy? You had everything before you adopted! We would eat with you at your restaurant, travel to the islands with you, and you were so much fun then! We never see you anymore. You are driving an old car, live in an old house in need of maintenance, and you are wearing hand-me-down clothes" (some they gave me!). "You are even cutting your own hair now—not that it looks bad—but you don't even color your gray hairs. Do you want to look older than you really are?"

I would tell them that when you really like your work, it is a joy getting up in the morning! I am able to bounce out of bed. As my feet hit the floor, I am off and running to a business call, or to rescue a pregnant girl in need, or to help a senior who needs shelter and assistance finding a safe place. Sometimes I'd bring them into my home until the safe home was found. Pregnant girls were sent to me by taxi from different churches, asking me to help them with the delivery of the babies. Afterwards I would find them a rental. There were no maternity houses in my area and it was quite a distance from two others that were usually filled to capacity.

I tell my "BC" friends that I love to read Psalm 92, which is written: "Your deeds, O Lord, have made me glad for the work of your hands! I shout with joy, how great are your works. To me you give the wild ox's strength. The just will flourish in the courts of our God still bearing fruit when they are old. Still full of sap, still green to proclaim that the Lord is just."

In Psalm 71: "You have taught me from my youth to proclaim your wondrous deeds. And now that I am old and gray, O God, forsake me not. I relate with joy when I recall: he will give the barren woman a home and bless her with children."

For sure in my old age, Our Father gave three wonderful children to one who was barren for 17 years. These three that he offered me were not only unplanned but arrived with perfect timing! His timing! Those three could easily have been aborted due to their mother's dire circumstances. It was He, the great merciful One, who forgave my very grave sins and lovingly restored me to peace and understanding. After traveling on that fatal highway, I realize that I too could have ended in an inconvenient pregnancy!

Now helping more seniors, I have been told by many that they had abortions back then, thinking it was just tissue. Some said they assisted with abortions for their children who were experiencing an unplanned pregnancy and now, with all the scientific research, they had come to realize that it was in fact their baby or their own grandchild that was extinguished in the womb. I try to comfort them, telling them that God forgives and to just ask Him for forgiveness. I tell them He forgave me after so many years of sin just as he did Mary

Magdalene! I considered myself worse than she. He asked her, "Has anyone accused you? Will no one throw the first stone? Then neither do I accuse you. Go and sin no more!" She accepted his forgiveness and followed him right up the hill to Calvary with the other women who had been ministering to him for those three years. She was at the cross with those same women and with Mary the mother of Jesus, and with John, the only apostle who stayed with him for those three hours of agony.

Mary Magdalene was at the tomb on Easter, looking for Him, and called out "Rabbi!" When He spoke her name, she was so glad to see Rabbi Jesus who removed her from the highway to hell, too! It is so wonderful that we have the word of God. I tell the seniors that the Bible is a reminder of the very words of God. It is a best seller of every year! I was told that the amount spent annually on Bibles has been reported to be more than one half billion dollars. I am not surprised, knowing how it changed my life and continues to be my standby guide. I consult it before making any turns on my journey now.

I received a very special insight when I saw what was written when Saint Peter denied Jesus three times. Peter was his right hand man! Peter, who had witnessed all of Jesus' miracles for those three years with Him, denied Him three times and said that he did not even know the man! What a grave sin. He knew Jesus to be the Son of God and that he had been chosen to lead the Church. Even he was forgiven his grave sin. I am the first to admit that I myself am capable of committing atrocious sin like Peter's too! I became more compassionate when someone was sharing with me their inability to ask God for forgiveness, as their sin was too great.

Jesus asked Peter three times: "Do you love me, Peter?" And three times Peter said, "Lord, you know I love you." The reply from Jesus all three times was to feed His lambs! When I find the need to repent, and after confessing to Him my sins and my sorrow for having offended Him—He whom I love—I feel the directive to feed the pregnant and the senior lambs.

After rescuing many pregnant and senior lambs, one account of rescue stands out. About three years ago while I was trying to renovate a small house to be used to rescue pregnant women, a very pretty young girl was referred by her friend to me. She had worked alongside her for years at a management company nearby. She was in the library on a Saturday trying to find out where she could get a late-term abortion.

She was making excellent money but school and work were too much and she thought she had to look for a late-term abortion. Her co-worker asked her what she was doing at the library. She told her co-worker friend that she was trying to find someone that would do a late-term abortion. Her friend was surprised, as she did not appear pregnant and there was no conversation with her at work about her being pregnant. Her friend, a Christian, said she thought that would not be a good idea. She knew her story about how she and her sister left home and went to New York to escape their home environment; they had an alcoholic mother who argued constantly with their father who threatened suicide. The two left at an early age and worked together in New York. She graduated junior college in New York and was now at the university trying to graduate with a degree in business. Her friend said, "Wait a minute. I just finished a job painting a small maternity home for a woman who just happens to live blocks from this library. Why not come with me to see if she can help you?"

Her boyfriend was in jail and he lost their apartment. She was living in her car and suffering from the heat to the point where she had to go to the emergency room for heat exhaustion. Her friend said, "Well, let's just go to meet Vera." I was at home when they came to my door and of course I told them that I could put her here. My home, as the little maternity house, would not be completed for a week with renovations. I told her she could stay here in the front library room and when the house is ready, she would be the first to live there.

I said, "I will move a bed into the library room and you can sleep here tonight." She said she would be back to do so at 4 p.m. I had to hurry because there was a lot to do before 4 p.m. I thought I should move my bed in there and put the library furniture in my bedroom. I thought: Well, I will just sleep on a cot I had on the porch for now. I then received a call from a church that I was helping to renovate. I told them that I was busy trying to move my bed into the library and move the furniture into my bedroom. He asked, "What will you sleep on?" I said, "For now I will just use my cot."

He said they would be right over and would bring a bed. "We cannot let you sleep on a cot!" They arrived with the bed and several men moved everything into place just before 4 p.m.! I thanked them and told them I would call them later about their church renovation. The girl never showed up. I waited until 9 p.m. and then called her friend who I had hired to do some painting. She said her pregnant friend called to say she did not feel comfortable at my house. She would feel better at the little maternity house. She said she would bring her friend the following morning to speak with me.

The pregnant girl said she preferred to stay at the maternity house. I told her that the renovations would be completed soon. I said that I would furnish a room for her when the renovators were completed so she would be the first one to stay there.

I pointed out that she could stay here in the meantime with her room right off the entrance.

I would give her a key to the house so she could come and go to as she pleased.

I told her I had a small dorm refrigerator I would move into the large library room and that a large closet for her clothes had been moved there already. She said okay and showed up with her things for the night. She did come in quite late and left very early for work. She then informed me that her boss was not sympathetic to her having to work in the heat outdoors, supervising management work, and would have to decide about what to do with the baby, as she had already been to the emergency room from the heat. She said she could no longer work outside managing the workers for her boss and would have to give one week's notice.

She said she was grateful for the room but she still was not talking much. She stopped me a few days later as she passed me in the hallway on the way to the guest bathroom. She had to pass my Mother and Child art gallery in the hallway going to and from the bathroom. She said she wanted to know who was the lady in the very large picture, as she pointed to Our

Lady of Guadalupe. She said, "She kinda looks like me!"

I told her that she was the famous Lady of Guadalupe who had appeared to the Mexicans who were sacrificing their babies to their pagan gods at the time. I told her that she did look like her! She said her father was from Mexico, but she never heard about this lady. I showed her the famous tie on the gown that indicated for the Mexicans that she was pregnant. She said no, she never heard of her, and was off to get her hair trimmed. I left for a church service—when I returned, she was there waiting for me. She asked if I had a moment to speak with her. She began by saying that when she went to get her cut with her Hispanic hairdresser of many years, she asked him if he ever heard about this Lady of Guadalupe. He said, "What! You are Mexican and never heard about Our Lady of Guadalupe!?" She said no, she had no knowledge of her, much less god. The man began explaining while cutting her hair who this lady was. He was Catholic and was able to tell her a lot about the picture and about God.

She started asking me questions about abortion. I did not get into religion with her, as it was obvious that she had never been told about God or the Ten Commandments—much less Our Lady of Guadalupe.

I told her that it was against the law to kill anyone—a baby or anyone for that matter. She said then, "How is it legal to abort a baby?"

I asked her if she saw the recent article in the newspaper about a drunk driver killing both the pregnant mother and her baby. He was charged with two counts of murder, it was reported on the local news channel. Another recent report in the news was a young man who did not want his child. In a heated argument, he punched his pregnant girlfriend in the stomach several times and the baby died. He was charged with first degree murder. She then asked again, "So why is abortion legal?" I explained that the practice now was to place a suction instrument inserted by a doctor into the baby's brain with the intention of taking out the brain material. The baby would be dead and would be delivered by the mother as such. This would be considered legal to give birth to the expired baby (at that time there were no states that were allowing babies to be killed after surviving the abortion procedure! There was no pill then either the mother could take herself that would end the life of the child).

She was silent for a long time. I just sat there quietly waiting for more questions. She said in a shaky voice, "Can you help me keep my baby?" She said she waited as long as she could to keep the baby, which was against her mother's orders to abort. She was not sure what to do and did nothing until her situation became impossible and her mother's urgings became hard to deal with. She said she wanted to keep the baby. She went on to tell me that before she decided to check on a late-term abortion, she had a list of names, and pulled it out to ask me what I thought of this name or that name. She said she liked the name Nico and hoped it would be a boy and Nicola if it was a girl. I told her that they were my favorite names!

The next few days, I helped her apply for Medicaid and then researched doctors that would take Medicaid. Since she was late term, many were reluctant and would not take her as their patient. I found one that would and she began prenatal care immediately. When the doctor did the ultrasound, it was a boy!

She was overjoyed and told me that she always wanted a little boy. She told me that she wanted to find a job now that her notice had expired with the management company. I told her not to worry and that I would pay her car payment and her cell phone. She had no maternity clothes and so we went looking. It was amazing that she still did not show as pregnant. She decided to settle for large shirts over some loose-fitting pants.

She found a job in a telemarketing office nearby. She said the large room was air conditioned, and she would never have to leave the office. She said she would be sitting down all day to make the required list of calls. She was glad to have an hour for lunch, which she would bring with her, and would be able to rest before going back for the second round of calling.

She was very intelligent and a hard worker. She learned fast and was earning extra money for her performance, signing up high numbers for the services she was promoting. This made her happy that she could still support herself. After she got home, I was glad that she went right to bed. With the baby expected to be delivered now in less than a month, I proceeded to find her a rental. She did not want to stay at the maternity house, which she visited and said she did not feel her room was large enough there to accommodate herself and the baby.

While she was at work, I went searching for a reasonably priced apartment for rent. I was successful to find a one bedroom near my house. I called and went to see the rental manager. It was listed that he would pay a commission and my realty company could collect it. I told him the situation and that I would forfeit the commission and to apply it to the security that was required. I gave him the first month's rent to hold the apartment and to apply my commission to the security. I would give him the application fee and credit score fee and any shortages for the security deposit at occupancy. The lease was to begin in two weeks. I told him that it looked like she would be giving birth before the lease began. I took her to see her apartment. She loved it!

She said it would be something she could afford and it was in a safe area. I decided to rent a truck and drive up to the faith farm, a 501(c) that sold all kinds of furniture and household items, new and used. I drove the truck there myself and chose everything I thought she would need. I found a crib, a dresser, a double bed, kitchen table and chairs, a sofa, lamps, and an end table. Also pots and pans, silverware, and a toaster oven! The prices were very reasonable! Faith farm loaded the truck and it was so full that they didn't think they would be able to close the large door of the truck.

They did a good job of fitting it all in and then asked, "So where is the driver?" I said, "I am the driver," and they gave me a look. (I was now used to that look! Those same looks I received for so many years.) The rental truck weaved back and forth and sideways as it was at full capacity. I drove slowly. I asked the church who had helped me with the bed to meet me at the vacant apartment to help unload. I had checked with the apartment manager who allowed me to bring the furniture in as the lease would begin soon. I gave him the balance of fees she owed and he gave me the key. Right on time, my little mother delivered the most beautiful little boy: Nico, with a head full of black hair.

When she said, "Here you can hold him" (I would attend the deliveries), I held little Nico, looking at his cute little face for the first time, I thought these little ones are priceless and worth all my efforts to support them. After two days she was able to leave and I gave her the key to her apartment. After stocking the refrigerator with food and drinks I knew she liked, I was glad that she could relax and nurse baby Nico. It was my custom to attend the deliveries at the hospital. I was at Nico's delivery and stayed as long as the hospital would allow me to.

When I saw her first nurse little Nico, I thought, wow, what a fantastic mother and child picture this would be for the art gallery! I thought I would just keep this memory to myself to be remembered and treasured. On to the next one now, praising and thanking Our Father for allowing me to participate in the caring of his pregnant lambs!

I rescued several seniors during this time. There was one older lady in her 90s who was renting with another 90-year-old woman when I sold the house. The senior whose family owned it wanted it sold. The owner's mother was to be sent to an assisted living in California. Her roommate, Mary, had nowhere to go. Her husband and family had passed. She never had children. I invited her to come live with us.

    During the time she had rented with her friend, she enjoyed going to the Elks club and went dancing there on weekends. She took her laundry out to be done by a laundry that would wash and fold the cloths. She played bridge every day with her long-time friends and went to lunch with them. She always brought back food for Brandon and Nicole; she was very attentive and they were blessed with a grandma! She would ask me to go to the Elks club down the street for dinner and dancing. When I said no thank you, she would say, "What's wrong with you? You are too young to sit at home." I was 51 then and she was wondering why I would not go with her. These were old friends of hers and it would be very safe. I did not tell her that I had my share of going out to lunch and dinners at my own restaurant. I thought, if she only knew!

When I sold the house where she was renting with her friend, I thought I was the winner on that one too. In addition to the commission, I got the best part! A doting grandma for Nicole and Brandon and Peter.

She went to bed most nights early. She did not watch TV and would take out her hearing aids, which was a good thing for her because these children of mine were very noisy! At the most she would eat breakfast that she purchased and then would drive off to enjoy her day with her friends.

I thanked Our Father for this blessing. She delighted in those children. She doted on Brandon and Nicole and Peter, bringing them treats. I so liked feeding His senior lambs, too!

Feeding the pregnant and senior lambs.
A single mom helped by many senior
grandmas and grandpas.

Grandpa John and Grandma Mary

Grandpa Norman with Nicole

Widow Grandma Mary lived
with us one year

Grandma Jill,
nanny for two years

Feeding the pregnant and senior lambs.

Grandma Claire
for over 30 years

Grandpa Peter to Brandon
and Nicole, father to Vera

Grandma Margaret and Grandma Inez
for four years

CHAPTER 13

Conclusion

I finished this last concluding chapter of *Desert Journey*. I was planning to send it immediately to be published by Leonine Publishers who published *Warrior's Witness* in 2020.

I asked the Holy Spirit for guidance before writing *Warrior's Witness* and heard the same caveat to rewrite it! I heard that I should rewrite the book and change it to the first person. Instead of writing, "He responded with these words as a prisoner of war," I was to write, "I responded when asked this question as a prisoner of war." I heard "hurry now and rewrite the book in the first person."

It took two years to write my last book *Warrior's Witness* because the warrior was paralyzed then, due to his war injuries and was not always available. I would tape record each chapter and then edit it. I would include it until all the chapters were edited and approved by the warrior. The last chapter was ready for his approval.

I was ready to take it to the warrior for his signature of approval and then forward it to the publisher when I heard: "Rewrite the book! Rewrite it in the first person." I called the warrior to tell him I was told that we needed to rewrite the book and write it in the first person, using his own words and write "his" own words to describe the emotions he experienced serving in three wars. The warrior would always comment after signing off on each chapter, "My goodness, you wrote that so well and accurate too. How did you do it?" I would respond that the Holy Spirit was writing the book, not me.

He knew I was counting on the Holy Spirit to guide me and said, "Okay," for the rewrite. I told him I would rewrite it quickly as per the instruction I received, still noting that I was to hurry to rewrite it and finish quickly! I rewrote the book and brought it to the warrior to reread and sign off on it before I would send it to the publisher. We both noticed that it was a very different book, using his own words in the first person to express his dramatic war experiences.

We were both pleased with the results of the rewrite. He died when it was being published!

I lamented that he never got to see the published book with its fantastic cover! Not to mention the excellent reviews. So this morning, having completed Desert Journey quickly, I argued, "Why am I hearing hurry rewrite and finish again!?" Am I going to die like the warrior did before the book is completed? Is that why you want me to hurry and finish this one too?

"Hurry to rewrite it and finish." Was I going to die from the Covid virus or from complications from one of my old-age illnesses? Maybe to hurry before my memory completely fails? The response was: "You need to rewrite Desert Journey because you never mentioned anything about your traveling for 15 years on the highway to hell! There's nothing about your rescue or your born again experience. This was the critical turning point in your journey and needs to be included!" I replied that it would be too embarrassing. I had never shared it with anyone! What good would it do anyway? Some would say, "Well, I never went that far on that highway!" I will be too ashamed! I heard this reply: "I am asking you to include your highway to hell experience, your repentance, and your return to My protection! More of My children are traveling on the wide road highway to hell! It has never been more congested! Please recount your highway experience and write how you were able to repent and return safely to My protection! I know it will be very painful, but would you do it for Me?" (the same questions I was asked for my consent to the third adoption).

I was absorbed with angst about how I could do this. I decided to just think about it and was in no rush to rewrite it! I then noticed it was time for the morning reading of the Liturgy of the Hours. I had heard that if you think you have received a challenging word from the Holy Spirit, He would repeat the word through another source so that you would know if it was truly the Holy Spirit who was doing the requesting.

When I opened the Liturgy reading for that morning, I was very surprised to find that it included an excerpt from *The Confessions of Saint Augustine*: "For behold, you have loved the truth, because the one who does what is true enters into the light. I wish to do this truth before you alone by praising you and before a multitude of witnesses by writing of you! I am thoroughly ashamed of myself; I have renounced myself and chosen you, recognizing that I can please neither you nor myself unless you enable me to do so."

I surely needed to be enabled to do so as well! This particular excerpt from Saint Augustine's confessions that showed up so soon and unexpectedly was indeed a quick confirmation! I began immediately to rewrite it and to include those embarrassing times when I chose to travel on the highway to hell and my subsequent born again experience. I was thinking that Saint Augustine's confessions would seem pale, a minor traffic accident, compared to my head-on collisions on that highway!

As I rewrote my journey, I realized that God had a plan for all His children way before He knew us in the womb! "Before I formed you in the womb I knew you" (Jer 1:5). "For I know well the plans I have in mind for you, says the Lord, plans for your welfare, not for woe! Plans to give you a future of hope" (Jer 29:11). I am hopeful to shelter the senior and pregnant lambs. Especially since I was just approved for a service mark (similar to a trademark) for intergenerational care for the state of Florida that would provide a crisis pregnancy home for pregnant mothers and their children. It would also provide an assisted-living facility for 130 seniors and accommodate those local seniors for day care who cannot afford the pricey assisted-living facilities in our area. A bus would pick them up in the morning and return them in the evening.

The third building is scheduled for a child day care center for 80 children and it will be affordable for those mothers who decided to keep their babies and other single mothers struggling to find day care centers in our area. This one will be run by the nonprofit. It would be open on Saturdays. Weekday hours would be extended to 6:30 p.m. I noticed in our area, for dog day care, there was an optional service for $150 a week to have their doggie bus pick up your dog in the morning and return your pet in the evening so that your pet would not be alone during the day! I decided to have a bus pick up the seniors who should not be alone either during the day and could socialize and dine with other seniors.

Assisted-living facilities in Florida are not required to hire a registered nurse. This one will have a registered nurse to monitor any emergency for the seniors as well as the children in the adjoining building and the pregnant girls in the crisis pregnancy center. I added the cost to the existing program. The bottom line was still showing a hefty profit! I don't think it was any coincidence that I was born at the Preston Retreat in Philadelphia (a nonprofit) for indigent mothers like my 18-year-old mother; there's no coincidence that just down the street was the Holy Family Center. No coincidence that I chose years ago to change the name of my 501(c) to the Holy Family House, Inc.

My desert journey brought me close to so many seniors who showed me what great things would come from writing about the healing and well-being that takes place when the generations interact! I want to answer that question again that I was asked 77 years ago in my mother's womb. "Who do you choose?" Saint Augustine said, "I too want to answer as he did. "I renounce myself, Lord, and have chosen you!"

About Leonine Publishers

Leonine Publishers LLC makes fine Catholic literature available to Catholics throughout the English-speaking world. Leonine Publishers offers an innovative "hybrid" approach to book publication that helps authors as well as readers. Please visit our web site at www.leoninepublishers.com to learn more about us. Browse our online bookstore to find more solid Catholic titles to uplift, challenge, and inspire.

Our patron and namesake is Pope Leo XIII, a prudent, yet uncompromising pope during the stormy years at the close of the 19th century. Please join us as we ask his intercession for our family of readers and authors.

www.leoninepublishers.com

www.ingramcontent.com/pod-product-compliance
Lightning Source LLC
Chambersburg PA
CBHW061426040426
42450CB00007B/921